D1152947

THE Luis Palau story

THE Luis Palau story

An autobiography as told to Jerry B. Jenkins

Pickering & Inglis
LONDON · GLASGOW

Unless otherwise identified, Scripture quotations are from the King James Version of the Bible.

Scripture quotations identified RSV are from the Revised Standard Version of the Bible, copyright 1946, 1952, © 1971 and 1973.

Scripture quotations identified NAS are from the New American Standard Bible, Copyright © THE LOCKMAN FOUNDATION 1960, 1962, 1963, 1968, 1971, 1972, 1973, 1975 and are used by permission.

Copyright © LUIS PALAU and JERRY B. JENKINS 1980

Pickering & Inglis edition first published 1981
by arrangement with FLEMING H. REVELL COMPANY,
the American publishers.

Hardback edition
ISBN 0 7208 0490 6
Cat. No. 01/1215

Paperback edition
ISBN 0 7208 0491 4
Cat. No. 01/1216

All rights reserved. No part of this publication may be reproduced or transmitted in any form or by any means, electronic or mechanical, including photocopy, recording, or any information storage and retrieval system, without permission in writing from the publisher. Printed in Great Britain by Bell & Bain Limited, Glasgow for PICKERING & INGLIS LTD, 26 Bothwell Street, Glasgow G2 6PA.

TO my wife, Pat,
Ray Stedman, and Dick Hillis

L. P.

TO
the Tony Martin family,
Aberdeen, Scotland

J. B. J.

Contents

Foreword

I have known Luis Palau for several years, and I have, often wished that someone would tell his story. And now, eureka! here it is. Best of all, it is Luis's own story, told in his own words, rather than by an earnest biographer far removed from the real emotions of the facts.

As you read the pages of this book, you are in for a thrilling real-life saga of an excitable Latin American whose character nas become well mixed with refreshing dew from heaven. And he is sharing that refreshment with millions.

KENNETH N. TAYLOR

Introduction: The Billy Graham of Latin America?

Few people remember where it started, but several years ago a free-lance journalist first referred to Luis Palau as the Billy Graham of Latin America. The label stuck, and though flattered by it, Luis is also embarrassed, because people could think that either he or his team was behind it. "I would never dream of drawing such a comparison to a man I have admired for so long," he insists, "but I don't deny that I have been following some of Billy's examples for years."

A quick rundown of the activities of Dr. Palau leaves little question that, indeed, Luis can accurately be called another Billy Graham. Just into his mid-forties, over the last two decades Luis has preached the Gospel of Jesus Christ to nearly 3 million people in 37 nations and has reached another 150 million via radio and television.

Luis has written four books in English and five in Spanish, as well as many booklets, magazine articles, and newspaper columns. His radio programs are heard daily by an estimated 14 million people in twenty Spanish-speaking countries. His team has produced thirty-nine Spanish evangelistic color films and four half-hour documentaries in English.

The Palau team is international, with members from Argentina, Australia, Cuba, Guatemala, Mexico, New Zealand, Sweden, the United Kingdom, and the United States. All over the world Palau crusades are characterized by their emphasis on mobilizing the entire Body of Christ through church planting and church growth.

More than Luis's preaching style and meeting formats have been compared to Billy Graham. Like Graham, Palau employs every form of mass media to saturate a city, and sometimes a nation, with the Gospel. Television, radio, the press, Bible literature, tracts, films, and one-to-one evangelism are part of the outreach strategy.

But behind this world-renowned man of God is also a husband and father. Sure, he's known as a fiery, even flashy, preacher, but he is also a human being with whom one can easily identify.

Luis Palau is quick to admit his weaknesses and failings. He reveals his battles with pride, anger, impatience, and temptation. Above all, his story contains an element common to almost every Christian's life: his long journey to peace with God.

Even after salvation and rededication and answering a call to ministry, many men and women live in fear and guilt and frustration, because they feel inadequate to live up to God's standards. This conflict clouded Luis Palau's early years, and, in his own telling of it, you'll learn of the intricate, fascinating events that brought an Argentine schoolboy-turned-banking executive into a ministry of international evangelism.

JERRY B. JENKINS

THE
LUIS PALAU
STORY

1

The Little Woman With the Big Facade

And their sins and iniquities will I remember no more.

Hebrews 10:17

It's a huge challenge to counsel people by telephone while all Ecuador could be watching you on television. I hardly knew if all the calls were legitimate, or if I was talking to someone who merely wanted to be on TV.

In 1965, when I was in my early thirties and had been a missionary-evangelist for a few years, a friend dreamed up the idea of a live counseling program in the HCJB-TV studios in Quito, Ecuador. I had a talent for thinking rapidly under pressure, but this program required quick recall of Scripture. It was good that I enjoyed studying the Bible and had done it for years, but now I was forced to go at it with a vengeance, storing up God's advice for the myriad problems represented by callers from all over South America.

The phones never seemed to stop ringing, once we were on the air. The program was called "Responde," and the people certainly did. Someone near suicide might call or someone who had just had a fight with his spouse or who had just been thrown out of the house. It might be someone who had been to one of our evangelistic services but who was afraid to come forward and receive Christ.

One November night in 1965 I received two consecutive calls, the first of which was one of the most rewarding ever on the program. The other turned into one of the most bizarre encounters in my entire ministry.

The first caller was a young woman named Ruth, who had seen her parents' marriage break up. She decided that if her father could live in sin, so could she. And so she did. Ruth tearfully told me her whole, sordid story of loose living and immorality in reaction to her father's similar life-style.

Now she was miserable and wanted to be forgiven. It had not been my practice to lead callers to Christ right then, but rather to show them from Scripture how they could begin to turn their lives around. Then I set up in-person appointments, where I could carefully show them the way of salvation in the privacy of the studio counseling office.

But this woman was desperate. When I read to her from the Bible that God loved her and offered His forgiveness and salvation, she wanted to receive Him right then and there. I hesitated. Did I want to do this on the air? Would it look like a setup? Was it a good precedent? It was obvious she was sincere.

I asked her to pray with me and added that anyone else listening in who wanted to pray along and receive Christ could do so. "Dear God," I began, "I know I am a sinner." She repeated each line. "I have abused my body. I have broken sacred marriages." And we prayed on, recounting the sins she had told me. "Father, I need Your forgiveness and Your saving love." It was a tearful, solemn, anointed moment as she prayed to receive Christ.

Those may have been some of the most effective minutes of my ministry. Potentially hundreds of thousands of people were listening in, and who knows how many might have prayed that prayer with us?

Ruth was so excited that she insisted upon an appointment the next morning, at nine.

The next caller was brief. A tiny, high-pitched, squeaky voice simply requested an appointment the next day, at nine-thirty. No more conversation. When I agreed, the squeaky voice simply thanked me and hung up.

The next morning, after I had counseled Ruth and encouraged her in her new faith, I walked her to the door and was leaving her with a Bible and some literature when I noticed a little woman walking through the gates of the HCJB property, followed closely by two huge, able-bodied men who could have passed for American football players.

As she entered the office, I asked if the two gentlemen would like to come in, too. "No," she said, "one will stand by the door and the other by the gate." It was the squeaky voice from the night before, and she was right on time.

She brushed past me and felt along the bottom of the edge of my desk top, as if looking for something. Without explanation, she moved to the wall and peeked behind a hanging picture. Her eyes traveled to every corner before she finally sat down. I thought she must be unbalanced.

She crossed her legs like a man and smoked like no one I had ever seen, man or woman. She attacked each cigarette, sucking every last bit from it and then lighting the next with the smoldering butt of the last.

In spite of her tiny voice, she spoke through a sneer, and venom poured out. Her voice dripped with sarcasm and hatred. "You pastors and priests," she began with disgust. "You are a bunch of thieves and liars and crooks. All you want is to deceive people; all you want is money. . . ."

She went on this way for more than twenty minutes, swearing all the while, and accusing, criticizing, insulting. Bitterness gushed from her and left me speechless. I had no idea how to react and couldn't have gotten a word in, anyway. I prayed silently, "Lord, how shall I handle this?"

Seemingly exhausted from the ordeal, she finally slumped in her chair like a jogger who has just finished a tough course. She took a deep breath, her eyes still flashing.

"Madam," I said, "is there anything I can do for you? How can I help you?"

She slowly took her cigarette from her lips and sat staring at me for an instant, then suddenly broke into uncontrollable sobs. I continued to pray silently, "Lord, what am I going to do? I'm no psychiatrist. I'm just a preacher. Why did You send her to me?"

When she was composed and could speak again, the edge was gone from her voice. "You know," she said, "in the thirty-eight years I have lived, you are the first person who has ever asked me if he could help me. All my life people have come to me with their hands out, saying, 'Help me, come here, do this, go there, do that.' "

"What is your name?" I asked.

She was suddenly hard again. "Why do you want to know my name?"

"Well, you've said a lot of things here, and I don't even know you. I just want to know how to address you."

She sat back in her chair and straightened up a bit. Cocking her head and looking at me out of the corner of her eye, she lifted her chin and took yet another drag at her cigarette. Then she said with finality, "I'm going to tell you," as if allowing me a real privilege.

"My name is Maria Benitez-Perez," she said triumphantly. I recognized the name as that of a large family of wealth and influence. "I am the female secretary of the Communist Party here in Ecuador. I am a Marxist-Leninist, and I am a materialist. I don't believe in God."

With that she took off again on a breathless tirade against me and all preachers and priests, the church, and anything else she could think of that rivaled her beliefs.

"Why did you come here?" I broke in. "Just to insult me, or what?"

She was thoughtful again. "I'm going to tell you my story," she announced. And for the next three hours, without pause or interruption, she did just that.

She had been a rebellious teenager who ran away from a religious school and was given a choice by her parents: return to school or leave the family. She left. The Communists befriended her and took her in. Within the next few years she married and divorced three times and had two children.

Despite her upbringing, she became a party leader and organized student rebellions. Her story was like the plot of a grade-B movie. I let her talk on and on, wondering when her first sign of vulnerability would surface.

"When my mother died and the bishop came to officiate at the ceremony, I just stood there and made fun of everything he did. I mocked him while my mother's body lay there in the casket. I made a clown of myself, and I've always felt a little guilty about that. Even though I don't believe in God, of course."

Every time she got onto the subject of God, she became enraged. She repeatedly rattled off her list of titles and beliefs and nonbeliefs. But just as often, she would return to the funeral of her mother and how her mockery of the priest still bothered her.

I kept praying, "When will the opening come?" Three hours after she began, we finally got down to business.

"Hey, Palau," she said. "Supposing there is a God—and I'm not saying there is, because I don't believe in the Bible, and I don't believe there's a God—but just supposing there is. Just for the sake of chatting about it, if there is a God—which there isn't—do you think He would receive a woman like me?"

So this poor, frightened, little woman with the big facade had a chink in her armor, after all. I had read years before that when dealing with a professed atheist, the best approach is to take one truth from the Bible and stay with it, driving it home until it sticks, repeating it as many times as you have to. The Bible says that the law of God converts the soul, not the arguments of men.

What verse suits her? I wondered. The Lord gave me Hebrews 10:17, one of my favorites, because it is so short and says so much: "Their sins and iniquities will I remember no more."

I said, "Look, Maria, don't worry about what I think; look at what God thinks." I opened to the verse and turned the Bible so she could see.

"But I don't believe in the B. . . ."

"You've already told me that," I said. "But we're just supposing there's a God, right? Let's just suppose this is His Word. He says, 'Their sins and iniquities will I remember no more.' "

She waited, as if there had to be more. I said nothing. "But, listen. I've been an adulteress, married three times and in bed with a lot of different men."

I said, "Their sins and iniquities will I remember no more," and began to count the times I repeated it.

"But I haven't told you half my story. I stabbed a comrade who later committed suicide."

"Their sins and iniquities will I remember no more."

"I've led student riots where people were killed. . . ."

"Their sins and iniquities will I remember no more."

"I egged on my friends and then hid while they were out dying for the cause."

"Their sins and iniquities will I remember no more."

Seventeen times I responded to Maria's objections and confessions with that verse. It was past lunchtime. I was tired and weak. I had no more to offer. I was at the end of my rope. "Would you like Christ to forgive all that you've told me about and all the rest that I don't even know?"

She was quiet. Finally she spoke softly. "If He could forgive me and change me, it would be the greatest miracle in the world. He can't do it."

"You want to try it?"

"It would be a miracle."

"Take a step of faith. Invite Him into your life and try Him. See what will happen."

Maria stared at me for a long moment and then bowed her head. "All right," she whispered.

I led her in a simple prayer of decision, confessing her sins, asking forgiveness, and receiving Christ. By the end she was crying.

She returned, a week later to tell me she was reading her Bible and that she felt a lot better. A longtime missionary woman from HCJB agreed to follow her up, but I was not prepared for what I would encounter when I saw Maria again, two months later.

2

Divine Ulterior Motives

Blessed is the nation whose God is the Lord; and the
people whom he hath chosen for his own inheritance.
Psalms 33:12

Back in Quito in January, 1966, for more television counseling and
radio-program taping, I was once again visited by my little revolu-
tionary. I was shocked. She looked happy and had even quit smok-
ing. But, despite a new bounce to her step, her face was a mess of
purple blotches and bruises. Several front teeth were missing, top
and bottom.

Shortly after I had last seen her, she told her comrades of her new
faith. At a meeting of all the Communist leaders of the country, she
told them, "I am no longer an atheist. I believe in God and in Jesus
Christ, and I have become a Christian. I am resigning from the party,
and I don't want to have anything more to do with it. We are all a
bunch of liars. We deceive people when we tell them there is no
God.

"Of course there is a God! Do you think flowers create themselves? Are you going to tell me that my beautiful babies are the result of some explosion in space a million years ago?"

It was as if she had let a bunch of hungry lions out of a cage. The
leaders fought among themselves, some trying to shout her down
and get at her, others insisting that she should be allowed to speak.

A few days later she was nearly run down by a Jeep full of her former comrades. And the next day four of her former protégés attacked her and smashed her face against a metal electrical box until
she was bloody and unconscious.

She was forced to hide out in the basements of evangelical
churches and in the homes of missionaries, always on the run. For
her and the HCJB missionary to be able to study the Bible, they first

had to drive around until they were sure no one was following them.

I was amazed at the persecution she had suffered as such a young believer. "There's going to be a revolution in June," she told me matter-of-factly. "We've had it all planned for months." I shuddered.

It was to be a typical Latin American uprising: students and agitators causing a disturbance in the streets, luring out the army, which would then be attacked and overthrown. The military junta would be forced to leave the country, and the chairman of the Communist Party for Ecuador would come out of his hiding in Colombia and take over the country.

Maria remained on the run until June. The Marxists' network of spies was incredible, and they tracked her down. Rather than letting them take her, however, she talked her four captors into taking a short break from their activities and going to her father's farm in the Ecuadorian interior, where they could rest and read a few books she had chosen for them.

Incredibly, they accepted her offer. On the morning of the revolution, the Communist Party leader came out of Colombia to talk to Maria. In a few hours he was to become the new ruler of the country, but first he wanted to talk to his longtime friend.

"Maria," he said, "why did you become a Christian?"

"Because I believe in God and in Jesus Christ, and my faith has changed my life."

"You know," he said, "while hiding out, I have been listening to HCJB radio on shortwave, and those _____ almost have *me* believing there is a God!"

"There is!" she said. "Why don't you become a Christian and get out of this business? We never had any real convictions about atheism and materialism. And look at all the lives we've ruined and all the terrible things we've been into. Here, take this Bible and this book [*Peace With God*, by Billy Graham]. You can go to my father's farm and read them."

Miraculously, he accepted her offer. Later that morning, the disturbance that was supposed to trigger a revolution fizzled into chaos because the leaders were off on a farm somewhere, reading.

Of the many, many people I have seen come to Christ over the years, Maria had the wildest story. It solidified in me a burden, not just for individuals, but also for nations, when I saw the effect of the conversion of one woman on the history of an entire country.

Though that was many years ago, the fire still burns in my heart. My desire since my late teens has been not only to see people saved from hell, but also to see nations influenced for the Lord, to live in freedom. Of course the Gospel brings salvation to souls; that's fundamental to my calling as an evangelist. But a Christian nation means the people will have better lives.

I want to see more nations turn to God, because it will glorify Him. I love to see nations prosper, and that is God's promise to those who come to Him. People can choose between a miserable life without God or a happy one with Him. What in the world makes millions choose the miserable life?

What drives me is the conviction that if only people would see the point and get the message, they would be changed. Maybe that's why I—along with many other evangelists—spend so much time literally pleading the case for salvation through Jesus Christ.

Even with my responsibilities as a husband and father and being the president of an evangelistic team, I find that I can be distracted for only so long from my burden to preach the Gospel to a lost world. I might be busy with business for a while, but then I'll run across something in a magazine or in talking with someone, and the drive deep within me churns anew, and I get anxious to preach.

It seems I have been preaching all my life; but of course I haven't. I wasn't even really a full-time evangelist until I was into my thirties, which is one of the ironies in a story that actually begins in the twelfth century, believe it or not.

That's when the Germans invaded northeast Spain and left a lot of blond, light-skinned progeny. Generations later, my father, Luis Palau, Sr., was born light and fair-haired, like most people in the fishing village of Cataluna. His parents emigrated from Spain to Argentina.

My mother, Matilde Balfour de Palau, was the product of a Scotish-French marriage, her father having served in the British Merchant Marines before settling in Argentina.

Thus, Luis Palau, Jr., born November 27, 1934, as the first—and only—male of six children, never really looked South American.

That is true of many Argentinians, of course. The big landholders in the country are Britishers who settled there. The railroad, the

ports, and the meat-packing companies were British built and became the largest industries. So many Europeans emigrated to work
there that they made Argentina more European than South American, in many ways.

So, how does an evangelical Christian preacher emerge from a
country where Protestants make up just 6 percent of the population?
Well, I'm only a second-generation Christian.

My grandparents on both sides were basically secular, in my
opinion, with the possible exception of my maternal grandmother,
who was devoted to the French Roman Catholic church. My grandfather always claimed to be "Scotch Presbyterian." If true, he should
have brought the Gospel with him to Argentina. (In truth, as I tell my
friends, he preferred Scotch to Presbyterian.)

My father's parents were nominally religious, as are many Argentinians. They were not committed to the state church and hardly ever
attended.

My father's dad died when my father was sixteen, so my father
was forced to find work early in life. He purchased a small pickup
truck and made enough money hauling materials to buy a piece of
land and build a house on it. He sold that, bought more land, built
another house, and sold it, eventually developing a thriving construction business.

My dad was a real entrepreneur in his own quiet way. He was a
man's man, self-made, self-taught. He didn't make waves; he just
made money. He was good at what he did, and he was a thinker. He
supported his whole family by building and selling construction materials, and, by the time he married, he was prosperous though not
showy.

My parents started their family in the small town of Ingeniero-
Maschwitz (named after the train station). Around the time of my
birth, my father probably would have considered himself a typical
nonreligious person. He would have said he believed in God and
Christ and probably would have aligned himself with the state
church. My mother was the churchgoer, playing the organ in the
local parish church.

She was searching for real answers in life, but she told me that at
that time neither she nor my dad knew the biblical Gospel—at least,
until they met Mr. Rogers.

Charles Rogers was typical of many British missionaries to South

America. He came to Argentina for the express purpose of winning people to Christ and planting local bodies of Christian Brethren assemblies, but he was fully self-supporting as an executive with the Shell Oil Company.

Many Brethren missionaries were European businessmen who had divine ulterior motives for coming to Argentina.

Somehow Mr. Rogers made contact with our family, probably through our Scottish connection, and he began carefully and quietly to cultivate a friendship with my parents until he was able to give them a Gospel of Matthew.

My mother was so hungry for God that she would kneel and read this Scripture portion. When she read the Beatitudes and realized that the pure in heart shall see God, she was convicted that she did not have a pure heart.

Mr. Rogers and his wife led my mother to Christ and, not long after, my grandmother, too, became a Christian. The Rogerses discipled them and got them involved with a few other Christians in the tiny local assembly.

My father said he didn't want anything to do with "this evangelical stuff," but those who knew when to look would occasionally see him standing outside the corrugated-metal shed, on the outskirts of town, that served as the Brethren place of worship.

Mr. Rogers and other preachers like him knew that some townspeople did not want to be seen in the building, despite the fact that they did want to hear the sermon, so Mr. Rogers turned off the outside lights during the sermon to allow shy listeners to stand close and then steal away before the service ended.

My father listened outside a few times before my mother decided it was time to get him into the chapel for a meeting. He reluctantly agreed, but if my mother had known what he was going to do in the middle of the message, she probably wouldn't have bothered to badger him into coming in the first place.

3

The Classroom of the Soul

And they said, Believe on the Lord Jesus Christ, and
thou shalt be saved, and thy house.

Acts 16:31

My mother will never forget the first time dad walked in and sat beside her in the chapel. And neither will anyone else who was there (except me—I was about a year and a half old). Mr. Rogers was preaching expositionally, as usual, and somehow the combination of what he was saying and what my father had heard during his surreptitious visits in the shadows was used by the Holy Spirit to work in dad's heart.

The Christian Brethren don't give altar calls, but dad wouldn't have waited for that, anyway. In the middle of the sermon, he suddenly stood and quoted a phrase often used among Evangelicals: "I receive Jesus Christ as my only and sufficient Saviour."

My mother nearly fainted. She hadn't expected him to make a scene. When he had made his declaration, he sat down, and that was that. He had believed and accepted and confessed with his mouth the Lord Jesus. And he was saved. Few times does one see such a spontaneous work of conviction, and I long to see it again and again.

With my father also in the fold, both my parents immediately became outspoken and enthusiastic Evangelicals. Because there were so few people in the church to begin with, and even fewer converts, the Brethren needed all the help they could get and had a way of pushing new believers into service right away.

It provided a perfect framework for growth, forcing my parents into Bible study and prayer, so they would be equipped to witness and defend their faith, especially now that they were hated minority Protestants.

They were baptized, and soon my father put his trucks at the disposal of the missionary. Every weekend a truckload of local Christians drove to different towns, to witness and pass out tracts.

Some of my earliest memories are of walking to church with my mother. She was so solidly converted that she was eager to stand up for Christ. I know it never happened, but in my mind's eye I picture her walking the family to church with a big Bible held high in front of her. She attended every meeting, and she never minded being insulted and called names. She was never ashamed of Jesus Christ; that I remember most.

When I was a child, there weren't more than a dozen or so people in the Brethren assembly in town, and that included Mr. Rogers and his wife and two children. My mother and dad, my two aunts, and three or four other townspeople made up our congregation, the only one in town.

It's interesting that I would grow up in a unique fellowship like the Christian Brethren. They didn't call themselves a denomination; in fact, they shunned all such labels, including *Brethren.* Their meetings were simple, staid, and sacred, with utmost emphasis placed on the Lord's Supper.

The movement, I learned later, was born in Britain, where many clergymen were not allowed to invite one another into their pulpits. They decided to minister simply to each other, in nonofficial but biblical, private communion services. It didn't take them long to realize that meeting with no denominational trappings was a vivid, beautiful portrayal of the Body of Christ.

To me, the Lord's Supper is still the greatest service in the church, and I like the way the Brethren do it. We sat in benches and chairs around the table, in the middle of the room. It's not at the front, so those serving the bread and the cup are no more prominent than anyone else.

There is no one leader; several men participate. In fact, there is no pastor. The leadership comes from within the assembly, even from my self-conscious father as he matured in the faith. It is simplicity personified. One stands and reads a portion of Scripture. Another prays. Another leads a hymn.

The communion service might take more than an hour, with songs and Scripture reading. But there is no exhortation or teaching. It is all centered on the person of Christ and the work of the cross. A well-known preacher or teacher within the movement might be visiting your church, but around the Lord's table, you are equal. In fact, they would rather that a prominent outsider not lead the service, so he doesn't give the impression that he's any more important than anyone else.

Around that table you get the feeling that, *Man, I'm one of the brethren.* The little old ladies who couldn't read or write were just as important as Mr. Rogers or Mr. Palau. I knew I wasn't one iota more or less important than any of the adults there; I learned a powerful lesson in my soul, which I never could have learned in a classroom.

During regular worship services, my mother pumped the organ. We children were always embarrassed, because we thought she sang too loudly. But she was always singing, even around the house. That memory blesses me even to this day.

I always thought of my mother as old, but she was just twenty-five when I was born. Frankly, she was plain looking, average in height and weight, with her hair in a bun at the back of her head. Everyone knew her as a kind, generous, and loving person. She was not loud or quick to laugh, but she was always gentle. My mother was never hard-nosed or unpleasant, but at the same time, she wouldn't let anyone's unbiblical comment go unchallenged. Her godliness has always made a strong impression on me.

Mother would not allow herself or those around her to talk about the future without adding, "If the Lord wills." It seemed a bit legalistic to us as we grew older, but she lived that truth. Some of our relatives even made fun of her, because she always delayed her decisions until she had a leading from the Lord. "Hey, Matilde," they would taunt, "has God moved the pillar of fire yet?" She took it well, but I didn't. I resented it, and I hurt for her, but it strengthened my conviction to follow the Lord. I find today that on important decisions I am just as deliberate as my mother was in waiting for clearance from the Lord. (Those relatives are all close to God now, by the way.)

She never missed a church meeting, and I admired that. I thought it was the way a Christian was supposed to be; of course, it was all I knew. When I compared her to other mothers, I did what most kids do: I decided I'd rather have her for my mother than anyone else in the world.

My mother read missionary stories to my sisters and me, over and over, before we went to sleep each night. My favorite was the true story of Mildred Cable and Francesca French, who carried the message of the Gospel through Asia in spite of tremendous persecution and physical abuse. That story would come back to me later and convict me of my need to share Christ.

Dad and mom also insisted that Sunday was absolutely sacred. No sports, no activities except going to church, resting, reading, or participating in Gospel street meetings in the middle of hot afternoons. Those meetings were often discouraging, but they helped mold my future.

I recall an active childhood in a happy home. Because of my dad's business, we had many buildings and shops and trucks and employees, including maids and farmhands. I'm often amused that many Americans think anyone who grew up in South America must have been a barefoot, poverty-stricken urchin. When I tell people my father was in business for himself, they say, "Ah, he raised cattle, huh?"

Like all the other kids in the area, I wore short pants—much to my embarrassment, because my skinny legs looked milky white compared to the swarthy brown ones all around. It was good that I was temperamental enough to defend myself when necessary.

My mother is easy-going, so I suppose I inherited my choleric personality from my father. I was exposed to his influence for only ten years, so whatever strengths or weaknesses I got from him had to be more genetic than environmental.

I idolized my father. He was everything I thought a man should be, even though he was quiet and humble for a man of such stature. I, however, had a quick temper. It is something that, over the years, I have learned I must constantly put under the control of Christ.

When I was a child, my temper flared up every time something went wrong or I didn't get my own way. I was persistent to a fault, moaning and groaning and pestering my mother for days, begging her to give in on some issue or another. In retrospect, I'm sure she was too nice to me.

As a child I was burdened with a tremendous sense of guilt because I couldn't control my tongue. I could shout and say the meanest things. If I felt I had been unfairly treated in a soccer game, I used some of the worst language on the field.

What always bothered me was that my temper raged over the little things in life, not the big ones. If I were the victim of another driver's carelessness, and he caused an accident, I could be cool as a cucumber. But let me knock a glass over, and suddenly I would fly off the handle. I am not proud of this tendency, but I would be a hypocrite to say it hasn't been a problem.

My temper flare-ups eventually caused problems early in my marriage, as you will see; but my wife Pat's cool head and appropriate reactions and God's continued dealings with me brought control.

I am a professional and a bit of a perfectionist. Seeming stupidity irritates me. Such anger is sin and can't be justified. But God has made me sensitive to the danger of overreacting, to the point where, for the most part, I can still handle situations quickly and decisively, while being careful not to overreact and insult or hurt someone.

Some of my old friends and mentors like to blame that part of my disposition on my Latin heritage, but good things, too, came from my unusual upbringing.

Many traits evident in me today are the results of other events during the 1940s, not the least of which were centered on my father.

4

Briar Bushes and Belt Buckles

Train up a child in the way he should go: and when he is old, he will not depart from it.

Proverbs 22:6

When I heard dad jingle his belt buckle, I knew I was going to get a whipping. He never disciplined me when I didn't deserve it; in fact, I probably eluded a few spankings I should have received.

My childhood was full of marble games, playing jacks, racing toy cars my dad bought me, and getting into all sorts of mischief with my sisters.

Once my sister Matil and I pretended to run away from home, when actually we were hiding under a sheet of canvas covering some bags of cement and sand my dad had stored. We crouched under that canvas for hours, giggling and holding our breath while my dad searched the neighborhood, calling and calling. We thought it was great, but that was one escapade that ended in the jingling of the belt buckle.

I hardly realized it at the time, but because of my father's business, I'm sure I had things better than most kids in town. I never felt like a rich kid, but even if I had, the daily put-down of being taunted by other kids as an Evangelical balanced any feelings of superiority. I was in the despised minority—a sign I sometimes wore as a badge of honor.

The badge I wore most proudly, however, was the honor of being Luis Palau, *Hijo,* or "the son." My dad was really respected in town, not just because he was a successful businessman, but also because he was honest. I felt that whenever I went into town for anything, I was greeted with respect because of my dad.

One of the things I remember dad talking about, even when I was a young boy, was that he always paid his bills on time and therefore had no debts. He wanted to die without owing any money. Maybe that's why I have such clear memories of always feeling welcome and loved in town. People called out to me in a kind way, making me proud of my father.

There was little I wanted that I couldn't have, though I think my dad was careful not to indulge me too much. I was thrilled when he finally decided I was old enough to take care of the Scottish Shetland pony I had always wanted.

The deal was that I would wash it, feed it, groom it, exercise it, and generally be in charge of it, and he would build me a stall and feeding trough and all the rest. The one rule was that my sisters were not to ride it. There was no way he wanted little girls to ride a skittish, bouncing pony. I was barely big enough myself.

I knew better, of course. Surely Matil was mature enough to handle it. She begged and begged until I gave in. She wound up in a briar bush; I wound up on the wrong end of the jingling belt.

I had had the pony less than a year when I went out to feed him one morning and found him gasping for breath. I couldn't believe it. We didn't even have time to give him any medicine. I was mad at the world and had to take it out on somebody. I wanted that horse back more than anything, and there was no comforting me.

I stood in a corner all day and cried until there were no more tears. I hardly ate a bite, and no one could talk to me. When I was finally too weak to keep it up, I ate a little. But I demanded to know if I would see the horse in heaven, and through that my mother was able to calm me down.

My dad became an elder in the local assembly and contributed the materials to build a new chapel. In fact, he supervised or did most of the construction work himself. The Brethren believed that plain was beautiful, and although I saw it as a drab Sunday-school room, with no pictures or figures and ornaments, I was impressed that my dad had built a structure for God's people, exactly the way they wanted it.

That room—while I grew tired of it and bored with many of the sedate services—had a positive effect on me as a child. The Lord's Supper was so meaningful and filled with long, silent pauses, that I felt we were truly all brothers under the cross, affirming our unity in the Body of Christ. And the fact that my dad and mom were part of it made it all the more significant. I'm sure much of what I learned and took from there is deeply imbedded in my being.

My dad was consistent, the same at home as he was in the chapel. He rose early on cold winter mornings to start a wood fire in the stove. I should have been sleeping, but often I sneaked out of bed just to watch him putter around the house.

If I watched long enough, I might see him go into his office—a little study he built on one side of the house—and kneel alone. Wrapped in a blanket or poncho, he read the Bible and prayed before going out to work. Though I was not even eight years old yet, I would steal back to my bed, feeling warm and grateful that I had a good dad.

One day he told me that he read a chapter from Proverbs every day, since it has thirty-one chapters and there are thirty-one days in most months. That stuck with me all my life, and I still try to practice it. I have told so many friends and associates that story that many, many people now do the same. In spite of all the other Bible studying and reading I do, I try to start the day with my chapter from Proverbs. And I have learned to do it on my knees, too.

I don't want to be legalistic about it, but there's nothing like studying the Word of God and praying on your knees. I have never shaken the habit of spreading my Bible and study materials out on the bed and kneeling to read and pray. It sure keeps your heart and mind in the right attitude. Sometimes it brings back warm memories of my dad.

Even though I had not yet actually trusted Christ as my Saviour, I knew my dad and mom were doing the right thing. When we rode on benches in the back of one of my dad's trucks and folded tracts to pass out in a neighboring town, I reacted to the taunts and insults with resolve. I saw the religious parades, common on the many holidays in South America, and I determined that one day Christians would do the same thing, emphasizing the Bible and salvation through Jesus Christ.

When a child is thrust into a position in which he must stand firm for the Lord in the face of opposition, I believe he is strengthened by it. It's much more valuable to our spiritual lives when we have to stand up for our beliefs in a non-Christian environment.

So I had an evangelical fervor—perhaps not for the right reasons—even before I was actually a Christian.

Much of my life revolved around going with my parents and friends from the church on little tent- and street-corner-meeting evangelism jaunts and helping pass out tracts, while Mr. Rogers spoke and others led singing or gave testimonies. Often the crowds were small or hardly existent, and sometimes we received threats.

Until Matil joined me a couple of years after I started, I was the only Evangelical in the local government public school. I was called names occasionally, even by the teachers, who made me kneel in the corner on corn grains if I misbehaved.

By the time I was eight years old, my dad decided it was time I went to private boarding school. Such schools were run by the British, and I think dad's main motivation was that I would become bilingual and thus have a better chance in life. He wanted to give me every chance.

My first three boarding-school years were spent at the Quilmes Preparatory School in Quilmes, about twenty miles south of Buenos Aires and a little more than forty miles from my home. My whole family went along on the ride to drop me off, and while it was considered prestigious to be sent to boarding school, I was scared.

To me the British were disciplined and precise, and I feared my poor English would get me in trouble right away. I could go home only one weekend each month, and though my grandmother lived not far from the school, I was not allowed to visit her or call her. When you're there, you're there.

I was one of only fifty boarders at Quilmes. Another two hundred or so boys and girls joined us for day school, and there was a homey atmosphere. With four boys to a dorm, I made friends quickly. But homesickness struck early.

I didn't want anyone to know I was crying in the night, so I pulled the covers up over my head and read my Bible by flashlight, not really reading, but just looking at the page numbers. I memorized the books of the Bible by studying the preliminary pages.

Eventually I began to enjoy myself and became active in all the games and sports and classes. It didn't take me long to improve my English, though learning it from Britishers gave me a strange combined accent—strange, at least, to Americans, when I first arrived in the States years later.

I did long for the vacations when I could be home with my family, and then I dreaded the end of the summer, when I had to go back. But Quilmes became my new home and was good preparation for Saint Alban's College, where I was scheduled to go when I was ten years old. I didn't know what Saint Alban's would be like, and I was glad I wouldn't have to think about it until the end of the summer (which in Argentina begins in the middle of December).

Shortly after my tenth birthday, I took all my final exams and began to make preparations for the trip home. A few days before I expected to be picked up by my parents, I received a call from my grandmother. She was not supposed to call me at school, so I knew something was wrong.

"Luis," she said, ignoring any amenities, "your dad is very sick. We really have to pray for him." I had a grave premonition, although she gave me no details. I had the terrible feeling he was dead or dying. The next morning, December 17, 1944, grandma came to put me on a train for home.

"It's very serious," she said. "Your mom wants you to come and see your dad."

The three-hour trip seemed interminable. I couldn't stand it. I wished I could have engineered the train myself. I really loved my dad more than ever before, although I had seen him so little for three years. We had talked and made a lot of plans.

But now I couldn't shake this ominous feeling. He hadn't even been sick, as far as I knew. Yet I was sure he was already gone.

5

The Palm of Victory,
Which Is Far Better

> ... I am the resurrection, and the life: he that believ-
> eth in me, though he were dead, yet shall he live: And
> whosoever liveth and believeth in me shall never die.
> Believest thou this?
>
> John 11:25, 26

I sat in silence on the train, staring ahead, yet seeing nothing. And
I remembered.

I was very, very close to my dad. He had always trusted me and
treated me like an adult, when I deserved it. His workers liked him;
his friends respected him; he was a good farmer, besides being a
good husband and father.

He may have been a bit too serious—seldom laughing or joking—
but having to support a family from age sixteen on would give anyone a certain sobriety and singleness of purpose.

Because of him I had many advantages over other kids my age. He
let me drive his new truck, sitting right there with me, of course,
when I was only eight years old. And he promised to buy me a
pickup truck of my own when I was sixteen.

He would let me crawl in under the hood and pretend to be working on the engine, when about all I could do was check the oil and
then try to get the dipstick back in. I was also welcome to sip *mate*,
green tea, with the working men during their breaks, feeling like a
man, treated with respect. That was one of the ways my dad showed
his affection for me.

Two years before, dad had given me a plot of land. It was less than
a quarter of an acre, but to me it was huge, endless. He taught me to
plant and water and cultivate vegetables and flowers in the six-foot-

deep, rich, black, Argentinian soil. Burned into my memory is a picture of him and me standing together among the corn and flowers we had produced together. If he died, I decided, I would never have anything to do with that plot of ground again, that special place I had defended like a castle, making people walk around it.

There was no way I could ignore the dread, the certainty that I would not be there in time to say good-bye to my dad. I didn't even know what was wrong with him. I wouldn't learn until later that he had suffered for just ten days, in need of penicillin, so scarce in South America in the 1940s. But something told me he was already gone.

I could hardly stand not being there yet. I've always been a take-charge type; even as an adult, sometimes it's been embarrassing. But it's part of my nature to feel that when there is a problem, I can solve it; I can organize people and get things moving. Here was a man about to die, leaving his wife with five children under the age of eleven and one on the way (Ruth). I had to get home and see what could be done.

I was out of my seat and pressing up against the door of the train by the time it rolled to a stop. I bounded down the steps and strode purposefully toward home. The blast-furnace-temperature air didn't deter me. It was the hottest day of the year, but to me it seemed wrong to see people lounging around, sipping soft drinks and fanning themselves. Something was terribly wrong at my house, yet people in town were lazing around.

Any shred of hope I might have harbored in the back of my mind during the long train ride was quickly dispelled when I came within earshot of my house and heard the traditional wailing. Some of my non-Christian aunts and uncles were moaning and crying and asking, "Why does God allow this? Oh, what will Matilde do?"

Relatives tried to intercept me as I ran through the gate and up to the house; I brushed past them and was in the door before my mother even knew I was there. And there was my father: yellow, bloated, still secreting, blood drying, lips cracked. His body had dehydrated.

I ran to him, ignoring my sisters Matilde, Martha, Ketty, Margarita, and all my other relatives. My father was still in bed, as if asleep. He must have just died within the past few hours. His body had not been touched.

I tried to steel myself in the midst of all the crying and sobbing, but I began to shake. I couldn't believe this! I would never talk to him again. He looked terrible, and I wanted him to be all right. I hugged him and kissed him, but he was gone.

My mother—stunned but not crying—stepped up behind me and put her hands firmly on my shoulders. "Luisito, Luisito," she said softly, pulling me away, "I must talk to you and tell you how it was."

She took me outside, and I tried to stifle my sobs while listening to her account. She told me that when the doctors had given up hope, they sent my father home. "Papito was yellow even then," she said. "That's when we tried to get in touch with you, so you could hurry home.

"It was obvious that he was dying, and as we gathered around his bed, praying and trying to comfort him, he seemed to fall asleep. He was struggling to breathe, but suddenly he sat up and began to sing."

I looked up at my mother, hardly believing what she was saying. "Papito began to sing," she said, " 'Bright crowns up there, bright crowns for you and me. Then the palm of victory, the palm of victory.' He sang it three times, all the while clapping in time, as you children did when you sang it in Sunday school.

"Then, when Papito could no longer hold up his head, he fell back on the pillow and said, 'I'm going to be with Jesus, which is far better.' " Two hours later he had died.

I turned that story over in my mind for days, even for years. It is still so vivid that I sometimes almost feel as if I had been there when he was singing. It was such a contrast to the typical South American scene where the dying person cries out in fear of going to hell. It thrilled me that my father was that sure of his salvation, and I never doubted that he was in heaven.

Still, my grief devastated me, and I was angry at everything and everybody. It wasn't fair. Why couldn't my father die in old age like everyone else? I locked the gate on my little plot of land, never caring to see it again. (I have never enjoyed working with gardens or plants since that time.)

It was hard to look at the buildings, the metal shop, the garages, and the work areas near our house. It hurt to walk by my father's little study. I didn't want to see anything that reminded me of him. There was no comforting me. My world, my future, had come to an end.

It was painful to mull over my mother's story of how my father had died, but I couldn't push it out of my mind. It was the only minutely positive element in the whole ordeal, and it has affected my ministry, my whole adult life. My wish and desire is that people get right with God, settle the big one, and die happy, knowing that they will be with Jesus, "which is far better."

Even our dog knew my father was dead. He curled up by the front door of the house and refused to move or eat for hours. He cried and moaned all day. The old-timers agreed that this was a dog that had loved his master and sensed when he was gone. It was many days before the dog perked up again.

Because there was no embalming, the dead person had to be buried quickly, usually within twenty-four hours. Once the doctor or undertaker had cleaned up the body and laid it in a casket, the Evangelical custom was that friends and relatives sat around it all night, comforting the family.

That was a horrible night. I didn't want to be there, and I didn't want to leave. I was a jumble of ten-year-old emotions. People sat around drinking coffee and talking in whispers. Since there would be very little time before the burial, relatives in distant towns were contacted and began arriving at different times all night.

Many found it hard to stay awake with my mother, so there were people sleeping in beds, chairs, and on the floor, all over the house. I tried to be an adult and stay awake all night, but eventually the trip and the trauma got to me, and I fell into a fitful sleep.

One thing I had determined, however, was that I would be at the grave site and would toss the first clump of dirt onto my father's casket. I don't know why it became an obsession with me, but I wanted to be the first to say good-bye after he was lowered into the ground.

It wasn't going to be easy, because the word was out that only the adults would be going to the cemetery the next day.

In the morning the casket was moved into the hallway in our home, and Mr. Rogers came to deliver the message. I don't remember much of what he said, but I remember the atmosphere, because in those days in Argentina, the Protestant missionaries—particularly among the Brethren—took the occasion of a death to preach the Gospel.

All the neighbors were crowded into our home, and Mr. Rogers spoke about the resurrection and the fact that Jesus Himself said He was the resurrection and life, ". . . he that believeth in me, though he were dead, yet shall he live: And whosoever liveth and believeth in me shall never die . . ." (John 11:25, 26).

At that point I felt complete assurance—even though I had not yet received Christ myself—that to see my dad again, I'd have to see him in heaven. Somehow I knew I would see him again. One of the songs they sang was "Face to Face":

> Face to face with Christ, my Savior,
> Face to face—what will it be?
> When with rapture I behold Him,
> Jesus Christ who died for me!
>
> Face to face—O blissful moment!
> Face to face—to see and know;
> Face to face with my Redeemer
> Jesus Christ who loves me so!
>   CARRIE E. BRECK

Even today, it's hard for me to recite the words of that song. I clearly remember how it was sung and the assurance it gave me that day.

Then death became, to me, the ultimate reality. Everything else can be rationalized and wondered about and discussed; but death is there, staring you in the face. It's real. It happens. He was there, and now he's gone, and that's it. Without doubt, the death of my father and the two days of mourning and burial had more impact on my future ministry than anything else in my entire life.

The smell of the certain type of flower that surrounded the casket nauseates me even now, nearly four decades later. But what seemed worse then was that somehow my aunts—the ones who were staying with the children while the other adults went to the cemetery—were trying to keep me from going.

We kids were all herded into the kitchen as the adults—nearly two hundred of them—got into the cars and trucks for the twenty-minute drive to the cemetery in Escobar. I was fuming. I knew exactly what was going on and became even more determined to get there and be the first to say good-bye.

This is my father, I thought. *And these people are trying to tell me that I*

can't say good-bye to him? Why? If anyone should be there, it's me. He's my
father. I loved him, and he loved me. And I am now the man of the family.
There was no way those people were going to stop me.

The trucks and cars were starting up. I was desperate. A bold run
for it would never work; there were too many adults between me
and the door, and they were keeping an eye on me, too. Everyone
knew I was upset, and they wondered what I would try to pull.

The first vehicles started to pull away, and the others were rolling
into line. I grabbed my cousin Robbie. "Distract my aunts," I said
frantically. "I'm getting out of here." He loved a good hassle and
nodded, smiling. I edged toward the window, where the shutters
opened out. Robbie sneaked up behind three or four of the girls.

Quickly he grabbed their hair and yanked hard. They screamed
and cried while my aunts charged in to pull him away. Meanwhile, I
scampered out through the window. Once I got that far, I was as
good as gone. There would have been a fight, if they had tried to stop
me then.

The line of cars and trucks was rolling away as I dug in and ran as
fast as I could toward the gate. I caught the eye of one of my favorite
uncles, Ramon, who was driving the last truck. He immediately sized
up the situation and nodded toward the back of the truck. I jumped
in and hid under some supplies, and when one of my aunts came
running out, demanding to know where I was, no one who knew
would tell her. I rode triumphantly, though tearfully, to the burial.
Now just let them try to keep me from throwing the first clump of dirt.

6

The Best Bargain

But I would not have you to be ignorant, brethren,
concerning them which are asleep, that ye sorrow not,
even as others which have no hope. For if we believe
that Jesus died and rose again, even so them also
which sleep in Jesus will God bring with him.

1 Thessalonians 4:13, 14

Since Ramon's was the last truck to arrive, we were a little late
getting to the graveside. Mr. Rogers was just finishing some remarks
as I got to the edge of the crowd. Several were surprised to see me,
the only child in the group.

One of my uncles gently put his arm around me, as if to comfort
me in case I broke down. I was just biding my time, waiting for the
right moment. Finally, several men began carefully lowering the casket. All eyes were on them.

I broke away from my uncle and shot through the legs of several
adults, squeezing past others, breaking through to find myself at the
edge of the grave. The six-foot hole looked so deep. Before anyone
could react, I grabbed a handful of dirt and tossed it down onto the
casket. It made an unforgettable, dull, echoing thud.

How horrible to be burying my father! When the shovels bit into
the pile of dirt and other mourners tossed in handfuls, I was grief
stricken. Yet the words about the resurrection and a heavenly home
gave me hope. He was still alive, and I was going to see him.

For days on end that summer, my mother was mercilessly pep-
pered with my questions about heaven and the second coming and
the resurrection. It was good that she had been a Christian for more
than eight years and had had fine Bible teaching in the assembly,
especially from Mr. Rogers. She had the answers I needed to hear
again and again.

She had her own grief and loss to deal with, and perhaps this was one way she did it. By reminding me and assuring me of the truths of Scripture all day, every day, she was probably simultaneously applying therapy to her own needs.

She drilled John 14:1–3 into me:

> Let not your heart be troubled: ye believe in God, believe also in me. In my Father's house are many mansions: if it were not so, I would have told you. I go to prepare a place for you. And if I go and prepare a place for you, I will come again, and receive you unto myself; that where I am, there ye may be also.

We memorized that portion, along with 1 Thessalonians 4:13, 14, which reminds us we have hope:

> But I would not have you to be ignorant, brethren, concerning them which are asleep, that ye sorrow not, even as others which have no hope. For if we believe that Jesus died and rose again, even so them also which sleep in Jesus will God bring with him.

The things of eternity and heaven became so settled in my mind during those few months before going off to a new school that I have never been ashamed to preach on heaven. Some people have become a little skittish about it in recent years, claiming that we really don't know much about it, whether it's literal or symbolic.

I don't believe we should go around mocking the streets of gold. Even if it *is* symbolic, why mock symbols? Scripture says the streets are gold, so let the streets be gold. When we get there, we'll find out what God meant. Anyone with any imagination should realize that heaven will be fantastic, if God depicted it as decorated with the most precious metals and jewels on earth.

I just can't imagine facing eternity or even losing a loved one without the absolute assurance of heaven and all its ramifications. To us it was thrilling, and through the years I have thought how lucky my father was to have arrived there so far ahead of the rest of us. He's in perfect bliss. He's happy. He's having a great time. He's in the presence of the Father and Jesus Christ. If I didn't believe that with all my heart, I'd give it all up.

I know my eyes shall see the King in His beauty. But you know, for years after that when singing "Face to face I shall behold Him ...," I never bothered to think of the *Him* as referring to Jesus Christ. I thought it referred to my father. That's who I wanted to see in heaven—and I still do.

Seeing the Lord Jesus will be far more meaningful than seeing my father, of course, but still I look forward to seeing him again. And it's just as real to me as if I said I was going to come to Los Angeles or London and meet you for lunch. When I got off my plane, I would fully expect to see you there, waiting for me. That's the way it will be with seeing Jesus Christ and my father when I die.

Malcolm Muggeridge says, in *A 20th-Century Testimony:*

> Death is a beginning, not an end. The darkness falls, and in the sky is a distant glow, the lights of St. Augustine's City of God. Looking towards them, I say over to myself John Donne's splendid words: **Death thou shalt die.** In the graveyard, the dust settles; in the City of God, eternity begins.

It's hard to understand why more people don't come to Christ just because of heaven. It's the best bargain there is. You give up yourself, let Jesus take over, receive forgiveness of sin, and are assured of eternal life with Him. Frankly, I cannot fathom the logic of people who know all that God is offering and still say they don't want to be saved.

People who know me best say I preach about heaven with more power and eloquence—not with human words, of course, but with a God-given sense of reality and passion for souls—than when I preach about anything else. I feel my heart almost bursting from my body in an attempt to draw more people to Jesus Christ.

A few years ago I was finishing a crusade in Nicaragua when a woman met me on my way into the stadium. She hugged me in typical Latin fashion and thanked me for presenting the Gospel so clearly that her grandson, Danilo, had received the Lord two nights before.

"The next morning he was so happy," she said. "He told me, 'Granny, I've got eternal life.' Then the next day he was run over by a truck and killed while delivering papers."

That story changed my whole sermon that night. I changed the title to "I'll See You in Heaven, Danilo," and I told that story just the way it appears here. The crowd was shocked. When I said he was out delivering papers the next day, they thought I was going to say that he was inviting more people to the crusade.

But I said, "Then a truck came along, and *pow!*"

Some thirty thousand people gasped, "Ohhh. . . ." They were as shaken by the story as I had been. Then I moved right into John 14. It was a fantastic night, with many people coming to Christ. In addition to the thousands in the stadium, millions heard that night's message as it was transmitted via satellite and shortwave to more than twenty countries. We also released a Spanish film of that message, and people are converted at almost every showing.

Some say it's wrong to appeal to people's emotions. Come now. We have emotions, don't we? God gave them to us for a purpose. If the story of the death of a beautiful ten-year-old boy shocks someone into coming to Christ, then I say, so be it. Praise the Lord. Let them come.

Years later people tell me that they still remember that night, whether they were there, heard it on the continent-wide radio broadcast, or saw it on the film. From death comes life. That's what the Bible is all about. Little Danilo did not die in vain.

Neither did my father, for his death forever changed my life and ministry.

I wasn't excited about going off to a different British boarding school: Saint Alban's College, southwest of Buenos Aires and part of the Cambridge University Overseas Program. But my mother said that dad had already decided to send me there, and she wanted to follow through on his wishes.

Meanwhile, my mother let my uncle take over the family business, because she had never been involved in it and didn't know what else to do. It would eventually prove financially disastrous, but none of us knew it then. We had always had all the money we needed, and I didn't have an inkling that it would ever end.

Saint Alban's was a tough, all-boys, Anglican school. The Argentine government required at least four hours a day, five days a week, be taught in Spanish. As Saint Alban's was a British school, they met the requirement and then taught the rest of the school day in English.

But we did not study the same lessons in English in the afternoon that we had learned in the morning in Spanish. We moved ahead in our courses. We became totally bilingual, and we got two years of schooling every year. That's one of the reasons the school was called a college, because by the time you were finished, you had the equivalent of four years of high school and four years of college and were qualified for *graduate work* at Cambridge University.

Saint Alban's was an expensive, exclusive private school. I don't mean that to sound snobbish, but that's what it was. Fortunately my father provided for me and saw the value in my attending. I became involved in all the activities, particularly athletics. I missed my mother and sisters, but with my father dead and my interest in his work and my land diminished, Saint Alban's became my primary home.

About half the students were British, the sons of railway, banking, shipping, or lumber executives. The South American students were from at least middle-class families, because of the cost. We all wore the typical British private-school uniform, from the youngest to the oldest. It consisted of gray flannels, and up to age twelve, you wore black shoes, long gray socks, short pants, a light blue shirt, a school tie, and a blazer. The whole school was divided into three houses: Corinth, Sparta, and Athens. I was in Corinth, but my best friend, George James—whom I had known since my Quilmes days—was in Athens.

This hurt, because it was considered treason to have anything to do with someone from another house. You could socialize with him, of course, but to cooperate with him in any way that might contribute to the other house beating your own house in games or contests was taboo.

The houses competed at every level. You could win points in swimming and cricket and all the rest. The points were tallied at the end of the year, and the winning house received awards. We all got up at the same time, made our beds and cleaned our areas just so, brushed and combed our hair, stood in line, marched, obeyed the masters, and were disciplined when we didn't.

We both hated and loved it. As we grew older, rebelling or putting down authority was the thing to do. Yet we were proud of our discipline, of our school, and that we knew what was proper. We had been trained to be responsible, and basically, we did what we were told.

We became closer than brothers, spending more than nine months of the year together. Perhaps not everyone belongs in such a boarding school, but for me it was basically good and healthy; and for the most part, I liked it. I hesitate to think what I might have become, had I not lived under that discipline and been expected to learn self-control.

Some of the older and more rebellious boys would run off without permission and buy beer, which they drank way up in the woods at the back of the school property. If they were told on, they would more likely lie than admit it, putting off the cricket-bat punishment for as long as they could.

There was nothing like having to bend over and touch your toes and wait for the swing and sting of that massive, flat bat. I ought to know, as you will see.

Though my grades were always pretty good, for a long time I had a bad attitude. My feeling was, "I'll study when I want to, and not just because the professor says I have to."

In spite of that, those were happy days for me. We had our fun with the teachers and with one another. Pranks, jokes, traps, anything was fair game.

The British were so well organized that the games and sports were really fun. It was more than a rag-tag bunch of kids running around and screaming and kicking a ball. In fact, soccer was considered inferior. There were teams and clocks and time periods and good equipment. I enjoyed it because it kept me from growing up too fast. And that was a problem.

With my father gone, I felt I got it from every side. My aunts and uncles always reminded me that I was the man of the family and that I would be expected to take over the business someday and take care of my mother and my sisters. I was just eleven years old, and already I had to try to decide if I thought I could do it. Even thinking of my father's business brought back the painful memories of his death. How could I run a business that carried such memories?

I began to realize that the business was no longer what it had been when my father was alive. Over the summer my mother began to worry about whether she could afford to send me back to Saint

Alban's. That nearly made me frantic. That was the world I really knew and loved. And it kept me from having to think of my awesome adult responsibilities too soon.

My mother wasn't even sure she could afford to send me to a camp that one of my teachers, Charles Cohen, wanted me to go to during school vacation. But she certainly wanted me to go. Mr. Cohen was one of very few Evangelicals in our Anglican school, and when he took boys on camping trips, they usually came back as Christians.

My mother knew I had not made a definite commitment to Christ yet, and she encouraged me to go to the camp. I didn't want to go, and I was determined to use our quickly deteriorating financial situation as my alibi.

7

Appointment in the Night

> See, I have set before thee this day life and good,
> and death and evil.
>
> Deuteronomy 30:15

Mr. Cohen taught trigonometry, history, and the Gospels at Saint Alban's. He taught the last particularly well because, though this was a formal religious course, he was excited about the Gospels because he was an Evangelical. He even hosted Crusaders—an extracurricular activity for Christian boys—in his home, under the sponsorship of the England-based Children's Special Services Mission (CSSM), today absorbed by Scripture Union, in Great Britain.

It had been after one of those meetings that he talked privately to me and asked me to come to his two-week CSSM camp in the mountains with some other boys. I didn't want to. It would be overtly evangelistic, and someone would put the pressure on me to receive Christ.

I knew the truth of Scripture, but wasn't really a Christian, although I knew doctrine and all the songs about death and hell; and if anybody asked me a question, it was easy to answer correctly and evade the real issue.

I told Mr. Cohen I would have to write my mother, and when he kept asking if I had written her yet, it forced me to go ahead and do it. She wrote back that she wanted me to go and that we should pray about it—clearly not the answer that was expected by me. I avoided praying and told Mr. Cohen that my mother didn't want me to go, taking two weeks out of the summer that were usually spent with her and my sisters. "And, besides, we're short on money."

It was a mistake to emphasize the money part of it, because that was all Mr. Cohen was waiting for. As soon as he sensed a put-off, he waited for me to paint myself into a corner and plead short finances, and then he had me. I had pretended to want to go, but that I couldn't because of the money.

He offered to pay, which intimidated me, in his typical, persistent Anglo-Saxon way that was hard to compete with. He wore me down, lured me into a trap when I was tired of arguing, and then had me. It was off to camp for me, despite my wishes. Even my buddies refused to go with me.

By the end of the 1946 school year (early in December, just before the South American summer), I had turned twelve and headed home for several weeks before camp began in February. It was annoying to have been caught and forced to go—which was not the "in" thing to do—but by the time February rolled around, I would be anxious to leave for the mountains.

My mother told me straight out that she was glad I was going, because she wasn't sure I was a real, born-again Christian. I responded, "Oh, come on," trying to pretend that I was. She knew better. An even more frightening experience at home made my dreaded soul confrontation seem like child's play.

That summer I was eager to get some proper instruction and information about girls, sexuality, birth, and so on. The older kids at school, especially the ones who went home every weekend, always came back with incredible stories about the sexy movies they had seen or the escapades they had been on with girls.

The full-time boarders were envious, even though we suspected we were getting an exaggerated and very distorted picture. It made me as curious as any twelve-year-old boy and maybe a bit more so. I just had to know what it was all about, and I hounded my mother for details.

She kept telling me that she would discuss it with me when I was thirteen, probably hoping that someone else would save her the trouble by then. It was too much to ask a widowed mother in those days, but I kept pestering her and pestering her. She would not give in. I wish she had.

I have always resented the fact that at no time—even during all of my teen years—not once did a Christian man take me aside and try to fill my father's shoes in the area of counsel on sex—or anything else, for that matter. I think it's an indictment on the church of Jesus Christ that we let fatherless boys and girls learn about sex from someone outside the church or family. Then many fail and fall into sin, partially because of their ignorance, and we are quick to condemn them (and abandon them), assuming they should have known something we failed to instruct them in.

Anyway, that summer my sexual adviser was a twenty-year-old worker who drove a truck in the family business. I was helping him deliver a load of cement bags and was really enjoying jumping in and out of the cab and feeling like a man. Then he pulled over to the side of the road and pulled a magazine from his pocket. At first I couldn't tell what it was.

"Luisito," he said, "since you are becoming a young man now," I sat up a bit straighter, appreciating the stroke to my ego, "and you have no father, you need someone to talk to you about the facts of life."

My heart began to pound. I was excited to think that I might get some straight answers from someone who really knew the score. "I want to make a man of you," he said. But instead of telling me anything, he simply opened his magazine and turned the pages while I stared in disbelief. I was shocked and disgusted, but of course I couldn't take my eyes from the page.

I had never seen anything that revealing. I knew it was all wrong; it was dirty; it wasn't pure; yet I was curious. I couldn't sort out my emotions. It was appalling, yet appealing at the same time. I wanted to see it, yet I hated it.

There were fifty or sixty pictures in his magazine. The fact that he would show me something like that shocked me. I couldn't even speak. If he had asked me the next day if I wanted to see the magazine again, I would have run the other way.

I could not push the images from my mind. I felt sinful, degraded, horrible. My mother would have died. I felt guilty all the time, especially in the presence of my mother or anyone from the local church. I was sure Mr. Rogers could read the guilt all over my face.

Impure thoughts invaded my mind. Of course I had all the usual daydreams about wanting to love someone and marry her, and as my sexual awareness was increased, I even dreamed of romantic love. But now this spoiled everything. I had been curious before. Now I was repulsed. And why had I not been able to look away? I was obviously perverted and sinful. I feared the judgment of God.

I was haunted by the idea that others might be thinking the same things about my sisters and my mother that I was thinking about the women in their families. My church taught holiness and purity, and my mother's holy life made me revere the opposite sex. Yet the impulses within me had now been twisted by what I had seen.

Not knowing that I was hardly unique among boys my age who had their first shocking encounter with pornography, I could not reconcile it in my mind. It was wrong; it was dirty; it was degrading; and yet it held fascination. I was in such a state that I was actually glad I was going to camp!

I had never been to camp before, so trekking off into southern Argentina to a hilly, mountainous area called Azul carried its own special sense of excitement. I tried to forget about the sins of my mind, because I got a dreadful feeling in the pit of my stomach when I thought of it.

At the CSSM Christian camp run by Mr. Cohen, I recognized several boys from Saint Alban's. We used Argentine army tents and brought our own foldable cots, which we set up ourselves. It was almost like the Boy Scouts.

We set up our tents, dug trenches around them, policed the area, and were generally taught how to rough it. There were probably fifty or sixty boys in all, supervised by Mr. Cohen and several counselors from different missionary organizations.

The counselors were all Britishers or Americans who were very concerned for the spiritual welfare of their campers. We had Bible lessons, singing, and memorization every day, along with the usual fun and games.

I missed the contact with the outside world. There weren't even radios so we could hear the soccer scores. No newspapers, no nothing. We were totally cut off. We were saturated with the Word of God and with happy, snappy Gospel songs, many of which have stuck with me to this day.

One morning an American Bible teacher spoke on purity in that ambiguous, roundabout way many Evangelicals have of dealing with the subject of sex. I didn't get too much from it in the way of the detailed instruction I needed, but it was very helpful for one reason. It was obvious that this man knew what he was talking about, and even as refined as he was about discussing the subject, his view of its sanctity and sacredness came through. More than anything, I was impressed that he himself was a pure man in an impure world.

I assumed that most people were as coarse as they boasted they were, and I still felt bad about my own confused thoughts on the subject. But this Bible teacher impressed me and gave me hope that there were indeed pure Christian men—men I could model myself after. Though I was attracted by the images in my mind, somehow I knew what was right. And this godly teacher affirmed that.

It was strange to see the stiff, curt, formal, aloof Mr. Cohen— whom I had known from Saint Alban's as someone above it all—in khaki shorts and a totally different setting. It was almost as if he were on our level, though I could never get that image of him to gel in my mind. He even acted a little differently, almost as if he had a sense of humor. The little jokes he cracked were incongruous with his station in life and his personality, and that made them even funnier. I was beginning to like camp, but I knew someone was soon going to confront me about my faith.

It was happening every night. Each counselor had about ten boys in his tent, and each night one boy was taken for a walk and given the opportunity to say yes or no to Christ's claims upon his life. By the second night everyone knew his turn was coming, because the first two kids in each tent were telling everyone what had happened.

If you really didn't want to receive Christ, they wouldn't force you, of course. This was a making-sure exercise. Many of these kids had received Christ, and the counselors were just helping solidify it and give them biblical assurance. Then there were the boys like me, who had grown up in solid, evangelical churches and knew the whole story, yet had never accepted it for themselves.

Even the unchurched boys knew the plan of salvation by the end of the two weeks, and many of them became Christians during those little after-dark walks with their counselors. It moves me to think how loving those counselors were and how effective that system was, in spite of its rigid programming. No one was badgered or forced, but no one missed his opportunity to become a Christian, either.

Finally my appointment with destiny arrived. I wished I could run and hide from it, because I was embarrassed that I had not received Christ yet; still, I would not lie and say that I had.

My counselor, Frank Chandler—whom I thought of as an old man, but who was probably not yet twenty—tried to rouse me from sleep. I had been awake from the beginning, because I was the only one in the tent who hadn't been confronted and I knew it was my turn. There was something about having to go with him that rubbed me the wrong way, even though I knew in the back of my mind that it was inevitable and that I would probably get the matter of eternal life settled once and for all. Still I feigned sleep and would not respond. "Come on, Luis, get up. I want to talk to you. Come on, up!" I kept my eyes shut and did not move. He shook me, then shined his flashlight in my eyes. He knew I couldn't be *that* unconscious unless I was dead, so he just tipped my cot over and dumped me out. I rubbed my eyes as if he had just gotten through to me.

I slipped on my canvas-topped shoes and put on a jacket. The night was cold, and a light rain had begun. We heard thunder in the distance and knew a real rainstorm was coming. Frank was in a hurry. I wasn't.

He walked me to a fallen log, where we sat and talked. There were no preliminaries. The rain was coming, and he had business to cover. "Luis," he began, "if you should die, do you know if you are going to heaven or hell?"

"Yeah," I said.

"And where are you going?"

8

February 12, 1947

... if you confess with your mouth Jesus as Lord, and believe in your heart that God raised Him from the dead, you shall be saved; for with the heart man believes, resulting in righteousness, and with the mouth he confesses, resulting in salvation.

Romans 10: 9, 10 NAS

"I'm going to hell," I said.

"Is that where you want to go?"

"No, I don't."

"Then why are you going there?"

"I don't know."

"Would you like to change destinations?" Frank asked.

"Sure," I said.

"Do you know what you have to do?"

"Yeah."

"What?"

"Believe on the Lord Jesus Christ and thou shalt be saved," I said. I knew it all and had know it for as long as I could remember.

"And have you believed?"

"No."

"Why not?"

"I don't know."

"Would you like to be saved and have your sins forgiven and know that you are going to heaven?"

"Yeah," I said with relief, nodding. I knew I had stepped over the line.

Frank pulled out his New Testament and had me read Romans 10: 9, 10: "'... if you confess with your mouth Jesus as Lord, and believe in your heart that God raised Him from the dead, you shall be saved; for with the heart man believes, resulting in righteousness, and with the mouth he confesses, resulting in salvation" (NAS).

Then he read the verses again, but dropped my name, *Luis*, into every pause, making it as personal as it could be. The Scripture was as clear as daylight to my heart, just as it had always been to my head. "Do you believe God raised Jesus from the dead?" he asked.

"I sure do."

"Are you willing to confess Him with your lips?"

"Yep."

I had already begun to cry tears of happiness. Frank led me in a simple prayer, in which I admitted that I was a sinner and asked God to forgive me. Then I asked Him to be my Saviour.

The rain was cold and getting heavier. Frank flipped quickly to John 1:12 (NAS) and said, "This is all the assurance you'll ever need: 'But as many as received Him, to them He gave the right to become children of God, even to those who believe in His name.'"

He prayed, and we hustled back to the tent. I could hardly sleep. I buried myself beneath the covers and, by the light of my flashlight, I wrote the date in my Bible, February 12, 1947, and "I received Jesus Christ."

I think of that night often, especially when people criticize speed and technique in evangelism. We worry about hurrying a person; but, I tell you, when the person is ready, get to the point and help him settle it. When you sense the Holy Spirit at work, time and technique can be irrelevant.

My mother was ecstatic, of course, which was opposite of the reaction I received from my friend George James and others at school. I wasn't obnoxious about it; I was so thrilled about my commitment that I wanted them to know. I even carried my Bible with me a lot.

I was more active in Crusaders, and the Anglican Church services we were required to attend weekly took on a whole new meaning for me. I was even baptized and confirmed. I joined the choir, until my terrible voice got me drubbed out, and I studied my Bible every day. I corresponded often with Frank Chandler (I still have many of his letters). And I became a much better student, especially in Mr. Cohen's Acts of the Apostles class.

The biblical classes became more significant to me, and I really studied hard and learned. I could visualize the cities and movements of the early church in the Acts, because it was so clearly taught. Years later, when I studied the same course at the graduate level in the United States, I found that I already knew most of it from that semester as a twelve-year-old, when I was immersed in my first love of Christ. There's not a more open and teachable mind than that of a child still excited over his conversion.

I felt closer than ever to Mr. Cohen and really pitched in to help at Crusaders. I sang out, listened hard, and studied all my Bible lessons. It was a beautiful experience and even alienated me from some of my friends who were still into dirty stories and other shenanigans.

That year our Crusader club was visited by two old missionary ladies from China, Mildred Cable and Francesca French. They had tremendous stories to tell of their travels through the Gobi Desert in the interior of China, of being dragged through the streets of the pagan cities because they insisted upon sharing Christ with the Chinese.

In spite of all the physical abuse and punishment and persecution, they stayed on for years in China, spreading the Gospel of Jesus Christ. Their witness hit me at just the right time in my life to make the best impression. I thought I had become an outspoken Christian, but what was I doing, compared to these women? Then I remembered that they were the very ones my mother had read about to me and my sisters when we were little.

I began to look for more missionary books and was inspired to read how men and women gave up the luxuries of life to minister under adverse conditions, just because they loved the Lord and wanted to serve Him. I prayed that I, too, would love the Lord like that.

I didn't know if I was going to be a missionary, but I really wanted to do something for God. I was getting the broadest background for it. I was attending one of the most "high" churches imaginable every week: the Anglican worship service. And I had grown up in what might be termed the humblest, most nonconformist church, the Christian Brethren assembly.

I feel I'm in a unique position to love and relate to the entire Body of Christ because of the diversity of my childhood training. From the most hierarchical of Protestant churches in the world to the least organized, plainest assembly, I was an excited, eager listener and learner.

One thing I gained from the Anglican Church was an appreciation for the beautiful language possible in prayer. I had been dissatisfied with my prayer life, seeming to just slip into repetitious blessings of mom and my sisters and my relatives. The Anglican prayers could be repetitious, too, but what a blessing they were if you let yourself think about their beautiful and deep content. One of my favorites— and one I use occasionally in my private devotions even now—was, "We have left undone those things which we ought to have done; And we have done those things which we ought not to have done; And there is no health in us."

The loss of that first excitement and love for the Gospel is something no one has ever adequately been able to explain. It happens to so many, and when I lost it, it was as if someone had pulled my plug and the lights went out. Perhaps I let a cynical attitude get in the way. Perhaps I ignored my mother's counsel to stay away from worldly influences like listening to soccer matches on Sunday and going to movies, and maybe I was succumbing to the pressures of my fellow students.

All I know is that one day on the way back from Crusaders, I carelessly left my Bible on a streetcar and was unable to get it back. With that loss went my daily Bible reading, my attendance at Crusaders, my excitement over Bible classes, almost everything that went along with my commitment to Christ.

I still loved and believed and respected the Gospel, but I did not let it interfere with my life. I did not totally understand this quick turn off, myself, but part of it may have had to do with a punishment I received at the hands of Mr. Cohen. He was the master on duty one day—a fearful role of disciplinarian that was rotated among the professors. I was in an art class and doing none too well.

I was showing off to some of my friends when Mr. Thompson, the new art teacher, recently come from England, walked over and made a sarcastic remark about my horrible painting of a tree. He was right, of course; it was terrible. But I responded with some foul word in Spanish, which Mr. Thompson was not supposed to understand.

"What did you say, Palau?" he said.

"Oh, nothing, Mr. Thompson, sir. Nothing, really."

"No, what was it, Palau?"

"It was really nothing important, sir."

"I'd really like to hear it again, Palau. Would you mind repeating it?"

"Oh, I don't think it was worth repeating. I—"

"All right," he snapped. "Go see the master on duty."

The class fell silent, and my jaw dropped. That was the ultimate punishment. No one else tells the master on duty why you are there. You must tell him yourself and take whatever punishment he deems necessary. I died inside when I saw that Mr. Cohen was on duty.

"Come in, Palau," he said. "Why are you here?"

"Mr. Thompson sent me."

"Why?"

He was being terribly cold, especially for someone I knew and with whom I had spent a lot of time. He was even a fellow Christian, but here he was, aloof and frigid again. "Well, I said a bad word."

"Repeat it," he said.

"Oh, I had better not," I said.

"Repeat it," he said.

There was no way out of it. I told him what I had said. He didn't move at first. He just sat there staring at me, obviously disappointed, but mostly disgusted with me. When he finally spoke, it sounded like the voice of God. He reached for the cricket bat—he was a pretty fair player and knew how to swing it.

"You know, Palau, I'm going to give you six of the best." It was the extreme amount of swats for any punishment. I froze. "Bend and touch your toes, please."

As I stood there bent over, he said, "Before I do it, I want to tell you this, Palau. You are the greatest hypocrite I have ever seen in my life." I winced. That sounded pretty strong. "You think you get away with your arrogant, cynical, above-it-all, know-it-all attitude, but I have watched you. You come to the Bible class, but you are a hypocrite."

That hurt almost as much as the six shots I took to my seat. The physical punishment stung for days, and I mean literally *days*. It was hard to sit down, and I slept on my stomach for a week. I cried and cried, as tough as I wanted to be about it. What he said and what he did were both good medicine for me, but it took years before I realized it.

For months I hated the man. I wouldn't look at him, let alone say hello or smile at him. I quit going to Crusaders, and I quit paying attention in his Bible classes. I went through the motions of going to church because we had to, but I acted totally indifferent to the services. And I was.

Something between God and me had been severed. Not my salvation, of course, but something sweet in the relationship. I started to stretch the limits that had been placed on me by my school and my mother and the church. At that time I believed it sinful to go to school dances or listen to soccer games on the radio on Sunday, or even to read magazines about car racing and sports on that day, but I did it anyway. I joined my old friends, began talking rough again, and in general developed a bad attitude toward life.

It doesn't sound like much now, but back then it was the height of shaking my fist in the face of all I had been taught. I had been an excited, eager, happy Christian for almost a year. And now I was flat.

I knew the Gospel was true, and I never once doubted my salvation, but my thoughts turned to what I thought were practical matters. The family business was failing; my tuition was being subsidized, and no one knew how long that would last. I could be out of school before I wanted to be, just because we no longer could afford it.

I could think of nothing more humiliating. I would rather have been born into poverty than to suddenly find myself in it, after having lived well—but poverty was just around the corner.

9

A Genuine Phony, Fast and Smooth

> For what is a man profited, if he shall gain the whole
> world, and lose his own soul? or what shall a man give
> in exchange for his soul?
>
> Matthew 16:26

Though I had actually cried when I lost my Bible, it symbolized a spiritual cooling-off period that lasted more than three years. I felt worldly and sinful and guilty, but somehow I couldn't come out of it.

I was frightened that I was falling away from the Lord, and I wondered what would become of me. I simply did not live for God during the rest of my school years at Saint Alban's and my summers at home. I knew down deep that I belonged to Christ, but to me the pressure to not be considered a fool was too much.

I stood by and let the two or three other born-again Christians at Saint Alban's carry the ball for the Gospel. Henry Martin and David Leake were two of the other confessed Evangelicals, and I always felt bad that I was hardly in their league as a witness.

Leake, now a bishop in the Anglican Church, didn't flaunt his faith. He was just faithful, steady. He never talked piously. He was just himself, and he was admired and respected.

Henry Martin, who now lives in the town I grew up in, was aggressively evangelical. He made a point of the fact that he wouldn't dance or enjoy worldly pleasures on Sunday or engage in the occasional beer-drinking escapades. He never hassled the masters, either, even when everyone else did.

One year we got so tired of the same menu week after week that we staged a mild rebellion. Everyone took just a few grains of rice and put them on his plate, leaving the huge serving bowls full at each table. When the masters came around and demanded to know why no one was eating rice, everyone pointed at his plate and said, "I had some! See?" Everyone, that is, except Henry Martin. He would not be part of any disrespectful actions, so he ate a generous portion of the rice. The others threatened to beat the stuffing out of him later, but he told them straight out that he didn't think it was right and that he couldn't go along with them in good conscience because he was a Christian.

Later they made good on their threat. As I stood and watched, several of the bigger boys beat him bloody. I felt so bad for so long about standing by and watching that happen to someone who stood up for the Lord that twenty years later, I looked Henry up and apologized. He forgave me, but he had totally forgotten the incident.

Over the years I've tried to determine just what went wrong with my spiritual temperature during those last years of school. First, I had no idea how to live a victorious life. Basically I had been taught well, but I was into a spirituality based on performance. I had no goals and little idea of my resources. I just knew what I had to do or not do to be a fine Christian.

It was a nice, mild form of legalism. Praying, reading, studying, and going to church can wear thin fast if that's all there is to your faith. I don't recall picking up any instruction on how to enjoy Christ, how to walk with Him and be happy in Him. How to really praise and worship God for who and what He is slipped past me, and I found myself bored with simply going on and on in the repetition of the routine.

Though I take full responsibility, three things contributed to my straying into the world. The first was that my father had not left a will, and my relatives who took over the business ruined it, leaving us destitute. I was not equipped to forgive them, and the rage I felt as a young boy is hard to describe. When I understood more of what had happened and how they had jeopardized the very survival of my widowed mother and her children, I felt I could have destroyed them.

Second, there was the lure of the world and non-Christian friends. They seemed to have so much more fun. I was drawn into a life of parties and soccer games and listening to the radio—hardly bad things in themselves, but they were indicative of my loss of interest in spiritual things.

Because of the business failure, my mother did everything she could to see that I continued in school. Since I was at least part Scottish, I was given a partial subsidy on my tuition by the English Aid Society. But I was forced to live with my grandparents in Quilmes and commute to school to save money. It was humiliating, and it also put me in a position to be less disciplined about whom I spent my time with.

Fortunately, even my non-Christian friends from my new neighborhood were pretty straight, or I could have gotten into really big trouble. We wasted time by sitting around and talking for hours, but what really made me feel guilty was spending my Sundays doing something other than Christian work.

My goals were to be a race-car driver, a soccer player, or a big businessman. Even though the family was nearly bankrupt and the business was virtually finished, I told my friends it was thriving and was just waiting for me to come back and run it.

I was going to be rich and powerful, a self-made businessman. Only I was lying. And it was during those really low years, when I was sixteen and seventeen and living with my grandparents, doing my own thing, that I actually blamed God for a lot of our troubles. I had come full circle from my first love of Him, to where I thought He had let us down.

Finally things got so bad financially that my mother visited me at school to tell me I could not continue much longer. I could finish what would be the equivalent of a junior-college degree, but I could not take the last year and qualify for the graduate program at Cambridge.

Completing the Cambridge program was a dream I had nurtured for years. Even though I was a rebellious student, my grades had been good, and I looked forward to continuing my education in England. Short of that, I at least wanted to go on to college in Buenos Aires; but that was out of the question. I would have to go to work to help support my family, and they were going to have to move several hundred miles north to Cordoba, now that there was nothing left of the business.

At this time my uncle Arnold Francken, who had married Marjorie, my mother's youngest sister, stepped in and kept the business together for as long as he could by letting it be known that he was running the place with an iron fist and a gun in his belt. He said he would shoot anyone he caught trying to steal anything, workers included. In the middle of the night he occasionally emptied his gun into the air in the work compound, just in case anyone got the idea he could slip past him. But, despite Uncle Arnold's iron fist and all our efforts, we ended up flat on our backs, destitute. I had been the victim of a cruel joke. Eight long, double years of schooling in the British boarding schools had left me with an intermediate degree, no money, and no future, as far as I could tell.

I still feared God, but I questioned Him daily and was sometimes glad that I had not served Him more. I felt He owed me better than what I was getting, so why should I live for Him? It didn't wash, though. All the while I knew I was wrong and that I should go back to Him.

I never made fun of the church, as some of my friends and relatives did. I knew better than that. But I went very sparingly to the Brethren chapel in my grandparents' town, and then only to please my grandmother. I went late and left early, doing my best to appear uninterested. It wasn't difficult.

I worked part-time for my grandfather in his small business of selling sauces and smoked fish to restaurants, and when my last year of Saint Alban's was over, I considered myself a real British man of the world. My six or eight friends from the neighborhood were from slightly outside the circle of my British contacts, but that just made me feel important.

I joined the local university club and bought myself a pipe. I studied a Dale Carnegie book and learned how to win friends and influence people by talking all the time about the other person and acting interested in any small detail about his life. I was a fast-talking, smooth-working phony, and inside I hated myself.

For one thing, I knew that my new friends, even those who didn't speak any English, weren't of any less worth than the British people I knew from school and the club. And try as I might to put myself in some aloof category of potentially rich and influential educated businessman, something at the core of me told me that neither I nor any full-blooded Englishman was inherently any better than anyone else.

That was the truth that had been burned in my soul as a child, when rich and poor, old and young, educated and illiterate sat as equals around the Lord's Supper.

My friends, though non-Christians, were really super kids; by most standards, they were straight. They never got drunk, though they drank a little. And what I considered sins—going to soccer games on Sundays, fantasizing about girls, and wasting time—were about the worst things they did.

They danced, too, but dancing embarrassed me—I felt awkward. I used these friends as an excuse to be more worldly than my conscience was comfortable with, but it wouldn't be fair to say they were bad influences on me. In truth, I missed my chance to be a good influence on them. If I had been able to communicate what the Lord could do for them at that stage in their lives, it might have made all the difference in the world.

But I wanted to be "in." I wanted to be cool. I didn't want them to think I was peculiar. The fear of the Lord kept me from going off the deep end and into any gross sin. Still, I was far from the Lord and ashamed to stand up for Him. In later years, even after I got back into fellowship with God, the memory of the way I shamed the Lord was a big cause of guilt.

The turning point came just before Carnival Week in February, 1951. Carnival Week is similar to Mardi Gras in that it is a week of total abandonment. Any business that was not crucial to the festivities was closed for the whole week. It was the week before Lent and would be followed by forty days of confession and penance, so during the carnival, anything went.

People dressed in costumes and masks and danced around the clock. It was not unusual for a young person to experience his first night of drunkenness during Carnival Week.

I had grown tired of the sophisticated little parties and games the university club offered, so doing something more bizarre with my other friends at first sounded like an exciting alternative. My friends and I made big plans for celebrating Carnival Week 1951. The more I thought about it, however, the more ominous it became.

Somehow I felt that if I got involved in the carnival, I could be severing my relationship with the Lord. I had already been ignoring God's ownership of my life and soul, and while, in my head I knew that nothing could separate me from the love of Christ, in my heart I feared God might not forgive this out-and-out mockery of everything I had been taught.

What would happen if something snapped within me and I went off the deep end? All the supposed fun I had been having for months left me bored. There was a discontent, an emptiness inside, and I knew exactly what it was. I just didn't want to admit it.

Somehow I knew that if I went to Carnival Week, temptation would overwhelm me and I would be engulfed in sin. I knew my mother and other relatives prayed daily that I would walk with the Lord, and the more I thought about it, the more panicky I became.

I had to get out of Carnival Week, or I would be swallowed up, finished, sunk. I'm sure the Holy Spirit was convicting me. Toying with the world was one thing, but abandoning self-respect and flaunting God's law was something else. I wanted no part of it.

There was no purpose in my life, nothing to look forward to except more of the same empty "fun." If I went to Carnival Week, I was convinced I would have gone beyond the point of no return. I had to get out of it.

My grandparents were gone that weekend, and the house was empty. The next day my friends would come by to pick me up for the festivities. I was beside myself. There was no way I had the strength to simply tell them I wasn't going. I had to have a reason.

Falling to my knees by my bed, I pleaded with God: "Get me out of this and I will give up everything that's of the world. I will serve You and give my whole life to You. Just get me out of this!"

10

Big Doors Turn on Small Hinges

Being confident of this very thing, that he which hath begun a good work in you will perform it until the day of Jesus Christ.

Philippians 1:6

I had no idea how God would get me out of my dilemma without my having to lie. I didn't want to do that. To prove that I meant business, I pulled my grandmother's Bible from a drawer and put it on the table beside the bed.

The next morning I awoke on my back in the empty house, staring at the ceiling. I stared. Then I blinked. Slowly I sat up and swung my legs over the side of the bed onto the floor and sat there a moment. I yawned. My mouth felt strange. I touched it. No pain, but it was bloated.

I stumbled to the mirror. My mouth was so swollen it looked as if I had a table-tennis ball in it. Staring straight into the reflection of my own eyes, I worked up a crooked smile. I looked the way you look when you come home from the dentist. "God has answered my prayer," I said aloud.

I called up one of my friends. "I can't go to the dance tonight, and I won't be going to the carnival at all this week."

"Come on, Luis! Everything had been planned!"

"No. I have a good reason, and I will not go."

"I'm coming over," he said. "You must be crazy."

A few minutes later he showed up with three or four of the others. They insisted that the swelling would go down and that I should change my mind, but by then I had a good head of steam going, and I resisted until they left. It was the beginning of the end of my relationship with them.

I should have told them that because of my faith in the Lord Jesus, I was afraid of the sin I might get involved in. That's what I would tell them today. But I was so spiritually bankrupt then that it took that fat lip to deliver me.

Knowing how good the Gospel is, I am ashamed that I was so cowardly. But at least I had made my decision, taken my stand, broken with the world. I went back into the house, broke my pipe in two, tore up my university-club membership card, and threw away all my soccer and car-racing magazines and many record albums.

The next day I went to church morning and night. The rest of the town, it seemed, was frolicking in sin. I was glad to have escaped. Everything changed. I was excited. Life perked up and had meaning again.

Looking back, I'm so thankful for the promise of Philippians 1:6: "Being confident of this very thing, that he which hath begun a good work in you will perform it until the day of Jesus Christ." Slowly I was seeing that although I might fail God many times in my life, He would never fail me. I would learn, step by step, what it meant to live a godly life.

I bought myself a new Bible and made sure it was in Spanish. I wanted out of the proud little world of people who thought they were superior because they were better educated and better-off. It was a difficult move for me, particularly because everything from the Bible and anything else of a spiritual nature had come to me in English.

It was time I started a career in which I could draw a salary and help support my family. Because I had been good in math and business, one of my former professors recommended the Bank of London in Buenos Aires, a huge, several-building, block-long complex with more than five hundred employees.

My British education and bilingual abilities made me attractive to the Bank of London, and I was hired as a junior employee in training, at a decent salary for someone my age. I loved being a workingman, traveling on the subway, dressing up, and working in the sophisticated, bustling metropolis I loved. Buenos Aires had 5 million residents back then. It looked a lot like Paris, with its boulevards, sidewalk cafes, and beautiful people.

Working there made it more difficult to break away from the style of life I now despised. The bank was full of office politics, the old-boy system, golf, tennis, card games, drinking, parties, and all the rest. All this irritated me. The pendulum had swung completely back for me.

I had gotten my taste of the world, but now that my family was living from hand-to-mouth in Cordoba, several hundred miles north, I had more important concerns. I dreamed of perhaps becoming a lawyer, of changing the world, of making South America a decent place for troubled, poor people to live without getting walked on.

I could discuss the subject for hours, and my friends and relatives warned me I was taking life too seriously. Perhaps I was, but I didn't think so. How could people play and party when others were going broke and being cheated and living in hunger? How could they ride around in golf carts, ignoring the lower class, when widows and orphans were begging for help?

I looked for the best way to change my world, and I wasn't sure banking was it, though I loved it in many respects. I was learning more than I ever had in such a short time, and I was a go-getter. When my own work was done, I went to the people above my level in different departments, causing them to be suspicious of my ambition by peppering them with questions about every aspect of their jobs.

I read the banking manuals in Spanish and English, learning the entire international banking system.

My best memories from that brief period center around the walks and talks I had with my uncle Jackie Balfour. He lived in the same house, and when I broke with my worldly friends, he and I would take a trip into the city at night and walk around. We talked for hours. He was very spiritual and just five years older than I was.

Argentinian cities were exciting in those days. Thousands and thousands of families jammed the walkways and shops, even as late as midnight. There was music and laughter and the smell of food. Jackie and I talked of what we could do to change the world. He was a writer, so we dreamed up a Christian magazine and even made mock-up dummies of the cover and page layouts.

Much of what we talked about and planned for that publication I saw become reality years later, when we launched *Continente Nuevo*, a magazine of teaching and encouragement for Spanish pastors. (In addition, we also began a Spanish and English news publication and developed a wide literature and book ministry. My staff estimates we have distributed over 12 million pieces of Gospel literature.)

I was full of idealism and ambition. There were things I wanted to see happen, things I wanted to do. Someday my chance would come; I was convinced of that. I wanted to learn, to develop, to make a difference in society. But first, I wanted to help my own family.

The best way to do that, in my opinion, was to get away from the old friends and situations in the Buenos Aires area and transfer to a branch bank where I could start over socially. And there was a branch of the Bank of London in Cordoba.

The only people I knew in Cordoba were my mother and sisters, but that seemed like more than I knew in Buenos Aires. Other than Jackie, I had no friends my age. There just weren't that many young people in the local church. I feared turning back to my non-Christian friends out of sheer boredom, and I had already resigned myself to the fact I would probably not advance far at the headquarters bank.

I determined never to compromise my faith, even if it might someday jeopardize my business future. I just wasn't "one of the boys." I refused to come to the drinking parties and the social events. I even avoided coffee breaks and instead went to the library. Still, I received a couple of promotions, mostly because I was bilingual, and I was doing all right with a little desk job, but it was time to move.

I knew I would probably be laughed out or even fired, but I decided to ask the personnel department for a transfer to the Cordoba branch. Asking for transfers simply wasn't done, but I had worked myself into such a frenzy over the state of the world and especially my own spiritual state that I didn't care. I was going to take the chance.

I filled out an application for transfer and sent it to the personnel department. To me it was a spiritual decision. I would not have been surprised if they had fired me. If that was God's way of getting me out of a situation He didn't want me in, I was willing to accept it. I called my mother and told her I had decided to follow the Lord. I couldn't promise that it would mean a move to Cordoba, but she was thrilled anyway and no doubt started praying for just that.

When I received a memo asking that I report to the personnel office, my resolve nearly went out the window *What a fool,* I told myself. *You've been an idiot! These people have been good to you, and now you*

ask to be transferred to some hick-town branch! Then I found myself slipping into the spiritual thought patterns of my mother and my resolve
returned. Even if the firing was painful and I had been stupid, I decided it was a sacrifice for the Lord, and He would provide.

"Why do you want to transfer to Cordoba?" the personnel manager asked.

I told him it was because my mother and sisters lived there and
needed me, and that I knew it had a good branch bank. I waited in
silence for his decision. "You know," he said, "it will be good for
you. You can learn banking much more quickly, because there are
only one or two people in each major department of a branch that
size, and there won't be the jungle of people to go around.

"In fact, we'll put this down as if it were our idea, and then we can
justify paying for your move and giving you a promotion and raise."

I was flabbergasted. But he wasn't finished. "If you progress as
nicely there as you have here, within six months we'll put you in
charge of foreign operations at that branch, and in a year we'll bring
you back here for a few weeks of specialized training. In our eyes,
you will begin as the number-three man in Cordoba."

I was not yet eighteen years old.

A few weeks before leaving, I was lying on the living-room floor at
my Uncle Arnold's and Aunt Marjorie's home, listening to an evangelist on HCJB Radio, though at the time I didn't know what it was. I
didn't hear the evangelist's name, but I heard him exhorting,
preaching, and calling men to come to Christ. Then I heard a beautiful man's voice singing a song by William T. Sleeper:

> Out of my bondage, sorrow and night,
> Jesus, I come, Jesus, I come;
> Into Thy freedom, gladness and light,
> Jesus, I come to Thee.
> Out of my sickness into Thy health,
> Out of my want and into Thy wealth,
> Out of my sin and into Thyself,
> Jesus, I come to Thee.

The whole program left me exhilarated. I realized years later that I
had heard Billy Graham and George Beverly Shea.

Still on that living-room floor, I prayed: "Jesus, someday use me on the radio to bring others back to You, just as this program has strengthened my commitment to You."

I've always believed that big doors turn on small hinges. I recognize a lot of the small hinges that the big door of my life turned on in my past, but one of the major ones was the move to Cordoba. It changed me. I became a different person.

I had been through a lot of new beginnings, but now I was taking charge of the family. My mother's influence on me would again be for the best. I would find it easier to live for God in a Christian home where that was encouraged and expected.

We were a big family, but we rented a small house because there was little money. My good salary didn't go far with seven mouths to feed. When I moved in, my family had already stretched the bedrooms to their limits. I took the living room as my bedroom, and the sofa became my bed.

I felt a tremendous responsibility to provide an answer for my family. I was still quite young, but life was a serious matter to me. Once in a great while some old business debt would be paid by someone honest enough to look up my mother and take care of it, but otherwise we had no extra money.

I had only a few clothes and made them stretch over a few years. I no longer looked like a banker, and soon banking became secondary to me. First and foremost was the family, and soon after I arrived I dived right into the middle of the local Christian Brethren assembly.

It was a group of about 130 people, probably the biggest local church I had ever seen and unusually large in South America at that time. They had an exciting program run totally by the elders and the one full-time missionary, George Mereshian. He took me under his wing immediately, because I expressed a desire to be baptized by immersion so I could become active in the work.

This was a very strict and doctrinally sound body, and they held fast to the rule that a person could not participate in ministry leadership roles unless he had been baptized, served in lesser capacities, and studied the Word in depth for years.

The Bible-teaching program was so sound and systematic that it was like attending a seminary. I was thrilled. I don't know where my hunger for the Word had been all those years, but when the elders and the itinerant full-time workers—we called them missionaries—

made the rounds with week-long studies of Bible books, I just couldn't get enough.

I began to devour commentaries and supplementary books by great Christian preachers, teachers, and writers. Books such as *Lectures to My Students* and *Treasury of David*, by C. H. Spurgeon; *The Man God Uses* and *The Revival We Need*, by Oswald J. Smith; biographies on D. L. Moody, John Wesley, Charles E. Finney, Robert Murray M'Cheyne; and the writings of F. B. Meyer, S. I. Ridout, J. I. Packer, Oswald Chambers, and scores of others influenced my life and ministry.

Many of these were precious copies of out-of-print editions, loaned to me by missionaries and national leaders. Today, especially when I'm in Great Britain, I eagerly comb the used-book stores in search of more of these precious treasures to add to my library.

For a year I was encouraged and watched while studying hard and performing menial tasks around the church.

I worked harder at my Bible-study program than I did at the bank, not because I was lazy at work, but because I had caught onto that quickly and moved up fast. When I landed the foreign-operations job, I found I could get my work done in a few hours and have the rest of the time to study my Bible and the commentaries, with permission from my supervisors.

I devoured that program, was full to the brim, and was anxious for some of it to spill out of me.

11
Am I a Soldier?

But seek ye first the kingdom of God, and his righteousness; and all these things shall be added unto
you.

Matthew 6:33

My insatiable hunger for the Word of God was increasing, and I
enjoyed trying to satisfy it. Then came the day we sang "Am I a Soldier of the Cross?"

I sang with the enthusiasm the tempo demands but hardly thought
about the words. The Lord must have used all the Bible knowledge
that was being poured into me to make me sensitive to Him, because
suddenly I was overcome with the meaning of the song.

Am I a soldier of the cross?
A foll'wer of the Lamb?
And shall I fear to own His cause
Or blush to speak His name?

ISAAC WATTS

The lyrics burst into my mind as if God Himself was impressing an
exhortation on my heart. "You sing of being a soldier of the cross,
and yet you do nothing," He seemed to say. "You have never suffered for the Lord; no one has ever said a thing to you against God.
Think of Mildred Cable and Francesca French—those two missionary ladies from Asia, whom your mother read to you about and
whom you met several years ago."

My thoughts turned to those cowardly years and how little I was
now doing, compared to those inspiring women. I could hardly continue singing. *What kind of coward are you?* I asked myself. *When were*

*you ever dragged by the hair or stoned or spat upon for the Gospel? You stand
here and sing about soldiers of the Cross, but you are no soldier.*

The rebuke did something for me. I took seriously the idea that all
this Bible study and training under the elders and Mr. Mereshian
was a call from the Lord to serve Him and even suffer for Him, if
necessary. It was then I knew that I probably wouldn't be a banker
all my life. I wouldn't be a lawyer or a judge, either. I couldn't
change my nation or the world through law or politics or sociology. I
was going to have to be a soldier of the cross or quit singing about it.

I had helped out in Sunday-school classes and dusted and moved
furniture and had done all the studying as enthusiastically as anyone, for a year. Finally it was time for my baptism. I was glad. After
that I was not restricted from any ministerial activity I wanted.

As a baptismal-day present, my mother gave me my own copy of
C. H. Spurgeon's *Lectures to My Students,* a book on preaching and
pastoral work for young preachers. That book molded my young life
and has marked my ministry.

Probably the most exciting outreach activities were street meetings, led by George Mereshian. We drove into neighborhoods, with
speakers on top of our cars. Someone started singing and playing an
instrument to draw a crowd. Meanwhile, Mr. Mereshian tried to find
an electrical outlet for his audio equipment.

He was quite a salesman. He always managed to charm someone
into letting him use a wall outlet in a house. Then we were in business.

My first speaking assignment was at one of these street meetings.
These meetings can fizzle fast if they're not kept lively. I was nervous, but I had prepared for days and was more worried about
keeping the crowd there than about whether I was saying everything
correctly. A lot of our workers went along to make it look like a big
crowd.

A close friend and I really started enjoying the street meetings. He
was a better speaker than I and could always get the crowd excited.
He had a lot of zeal. It was great to plan for these little junkets, but
we didn't see many conversions. The training was more beneficial to
us and our future ministries than it was to the populace.

The first time I spoke formally in the Brethren assembly was at a
youth meeting, which was customarily also attended by adults.

There was a crowd of 120, including my beaming relatives. I was scared to death.

I had studied Spurgeon's notes on Psalm 1 from *The Treasury of David* for weeks on my knees. I prayed and prayed. For some reason, knowing that everyone in the audience was at least as accomplished a Bible student as I was made this kind of a speaking engagement more frightening than preaching on the street.

It was more than just the delivery of a sermon. It was supposed to be a message from God—which it was—though it came through the lips and pen of C. H. Spurgeon. Still, God had impressed it upon me to preach it, too. I thought I was ready, but I dreaded going through with it.

It was all I could do to talk myself into showing up, but I had my outline and my notes prepared. I figured I was ready with about forty minutes' worth of thoughts and hoped I wouldn't go over my time allotment.

I needn't have worried. My throat was dry. The butterflies never stopped. I practically read my notes verbatim and finished in eleven minutes and a few seconds.

I felt I had failed, even though Spurgeon's thoughts were good. More than anything, I was relieved it was over.

Meanwhile, the financial situation at home wasn't getting any better. The Lord had impressed upon me to take care of my mother and sisters, and He would take care of me. And He did. While we sometimes ate a loaf of French bread with a little garlic for our whole meal, I wore my Uncle Arnold's discarded suits and my grandfather's old topcoats.

This didn't bother me. I was in the Word and had shaken many of my fears of not being accepted or part of the crowd. I still worked hard at the bank and kept advancing, but the money just didn't stretch far with my five sisters growing up.

I knew God meant it for our good. We had been wealthy, so poverty was an education. I understand and love the poor so much better now because I have been there. It would have been difficult had I simply been raised in British boarding schools and lived in wealth until landing a job. It taught me to walk humbly before the Lord and to look to Him for everything. There was nowhere else to look.

My mother never lost her spiritual sensitivity. She knew it was a blessed experience to trust the Lord for day-to-day provisions. She often quoted Scripture to us during those rough times, and we all grew from it.

Matthew 6:33 was a reality to us day by day, "But seek ye first the kingdom of God, and his righteousness; and all these things shall be added unto you."

At the bank my co-workers began to call me the Pastor. While I was now in a position of influence at work and in the community, I no longer denied I was a Christian as I had done in earlier years. I was associating with wealthy people, but they all knew of my faith.

I still found more and more time, even at the office, to study theology. I studied whole books of the Bible like *Jeremiah* by F. B. Meyer. I read through Bible commentaries such as Jamieson, Fausset, and Brown on the New Testament, and Bible dictionaries. I studied up to five different subjects a week.

I kept reading and reading and accepting more opportunities to preach and teach at churches, youth meetings, and on the street. I couldn't have studied more or harder or faster if I had been in seminary. In a way I was in seminary. For two years, George Mereshian discipled me three hours a day, three days a week.

At his house we'd kneel in front of his couch and read the Scriptures. He then explained it and answered my questions. We looked up the comments by men of God on the passage. We covered a lot of ground in that time. I learned as much from this humble, holy man as I did from the study itself.

I became the Sunday-school superintendent and learned to organize workers and programs. I was tough, too. If the teachers couldn't make it to the teachers' meetings, they couldn't teach on Sundays. No exceptions.

By the time I was into my early twenties, the elders felt that many of us young men could handle the street work by ourselves. My friend and I headed up a team that really made the rounds. We preached all over the place, taking turns drawing the crowd and leading the singing and then preaching.

Interestingly enough, though I loved to preach and felt burdened to invite people to turn to Christ, my friend was considered the evangelist. People said we made a great team and that I should be the Bible teacher and he the evangelist. And that's the way it was for a while.

If it was an evangelistic service, I emceed the meeting, and he preached. If the emphasis was on exposition or doctrine or theology, he led the meeting, and I taught. I learned a lot from him. He had tremendous voice projection, was a good musician and singer, and was very entertaining. We traveled to little chapels all over the countryside and continued our street meetings.

That's really where I began to learn the basics of evangelism. You run into everything when you preach on the street: laughter, scorn, hecklers, questions that require quick answers, questions that require diplomacy, all kinds of things. One thing burned into our minds by the elders was that we had the truth. We stood on the truth. There was nothing that could stop the power of the Word of God. You can afford to let hecklers and arguers talk their heads off, because when you respond with the Word of God, you slay them. Truth is truth, and any honest person who hears it knows it.

In *The Joyful Christian*, C. S. Lewis is quoted: "The great difficulty is to get modern audiences to realize that you are preaching Christianity solely and simply because you happen to think it *true*; they always suppose you are preaching it because you like it or think it good for society or something of that sort. . . ."

My young evangelist friend and I challenged each other to get up early in the morning to pray. He lived a few blocks away, and we traded off meeting at each other's house at 5:00 A.M. Gradually more and more of our young friends joined us for Bible studies and prayer. They were committed. They meant business.

Every Friday night we were committed to spending the entire night in prayer. We had cookies and coffee to help keep us awake, and the whole purpose was to help one another, encourage one another, confess our sins, find escapes from temptation, and stay on top spiritually.

We even developed a midday seven-minute radio program called "Christian Meditation," which was aired locally just after the one-o'clock news every day. My responsibility was to write the message and present it every other day. That was the beginning of what would become an extensive broadcast-media involvement for me, but back then I figured that would be the extent of it. I was developing an overwhelming desire to win people and nations to Christ, but I didn't know where it would lead.

The other young fellows and I were working in Sunday schools, street meetings, youth meetings, selling Bibles, handing out tracts. The church was really hopping. Nevertheless, even with all that activity, few of us knew yet what true victory in the Spirit was.

We had doctrine, but some of us never did seem to get the point of what it is to walk in the Spirit and not be legalistic. I longed to walk in the power of the Spirit and be free of the self-effort of the flesh. Discipline is good, but in the frenzy of activity I found little sense of victory or powerful living.

Our times of study and prayer and work became a cycle of grim determination to stay with it, to keep on keeping on. We knew the power was to come from the Spirit, but for some reason we weren't experiencing it. We continued to search desperately, when we should have long since found it.

Though we were ahead of most people our age in serving the Lord, we desperately needed to know how to rely on the indwelling Christ and not on our own efforts. Many of the guys eventually dropped out, tired of the battle. I was on the verge myself, not because I saw any lack in God, but because I was weary of fighting and struggling and seeking on my own to persevere through sheer dedication. I was exhausted, and exhaustion can breed cynicism.

When was I ever going to catch on? Would I give up now, after all I'd been through? I knew the other side of life was hopeless. But there is a monumental emptiness when you know you're looking in the right place and still are not finding the answer.

I wanted victory. I wanted peace. I wanted to rest in Jesus, instead of wrestling with Him. I agonized literally whole nights in prayer, seeking God's power and fire and ability. I wanted to please and love and serve God; I wanted people saved. I would sing "Oh, Jesus I have promised to serve Thee to the end," and I would think, *Even if it kills me.* It was a gritting-your-teeth kind of hanging in there.

I didn't know how much longer I could take it.

12
Emerging From the Wilderness

Go therefore and make disciples of all nations, bap-
tizing them in the name of the Father and of the Son
and of the Holy Spirit.

Matthew 28:19 RSV

I kept trying new programs for the Sunday school and our other ministries, trying to shake loose from the small-potatoes types of results we had been having. Many of the ideas came from reading materials I got from the United States, including a whole new concept—to me—that I picked up from a Southern Baptist publication. The idea? Daily Vacation Bible School.

A Southern Baptist missionary put me onto many fine Sunday-school magazines, including one that was great for the superintendent, and some Nazarene publications. The Southern Baptists were so organized that I was inspired to learn management principles. Our teachers, even those who did not have high-school educations, found themselves studying child psychology and pedagogy.

I knew it was important and would work, because before I had even become Sunday-school superintendent, I had taken training with Child Evangelism Fellowship. Two single women in their mid-thirties—Theda Krieger and Margaret Tyson—with CEF showed such love to children and belief in training classes that I talked a group of friends and my sisters into attending their training sessions with me. After learning how to prepare lessons, give an introduction, tell a story, work in the Scripture, and lead someone to Christ, I was ready to really get rolling in Vacation Bible School.

Paying for it ourselves, several of us young people bused young-sters from all over the area to a country spot where we held VBS. I directed it and also taught a class of about ten boys aged ten to twelve. When three of them came to Christ by the end of the week, I had developed such a passion for souls that I was ready to burst. This passion for the lost, fanned into flames as we led these young-sters to Christ, has never diminished. Today, as I see the hundreds of people responding to crusade invitations, I get so excited to realize God is using us to fulfill the Great Commission:

> Go therefore and make disciples of all nations, baptizing them in the name of the Father and of the Son and of the Holy Spirit, teaching them to observe all that I have commanded you; and lo, I am with you always, to the close of the age.
>
> RSV

Nothing is more thrilling.

All my church work and study took on a different flavor. In the midst of it all, however, there was far too much backbiting and criti-cizing of other Christians, other denominations, and even other churches within the group. It was what I call a certain unvictory.

It wasn't only among us young adults. We saw it in the older peo-ple. Envy, pride, divisive spirits. Also the temptation to fall into im-morality was almost unbearable. We had hoped that being active Christians would somehow diminish the normal thought-life temp-tations that face young men. It didn't happen. We were expecting more than the Bible promised.

All during that time I struggled with the question of whether I was too big a scoundrel for the Lord to work with. Perhaps I was so base that He couldn't give me victory, because I would mess up. I was hot and cold at the same time. I loved God, and I was burdened to share Christ, but I still longed for that inner peace, that feeling of resting in Him even while working hard and fast to spread the Gospel.

Unfortunately, most of the key men in our young-people's group dropped out under the same burden. Others joined us, but I have al-ways felt bad that the original core of committed young men broke up after about two years.

I weighed the whole matter for several days, seeking the Lord in prayer. I wound up still frustrated, still short of what I felt the Scripture offered in terms of peace and God and victory and purity in my thought life. Until I found the answer, I would not quit looking for it. Neither would I allow the search for my own victory to get in the way of offering God's love and salvation to people who had a greater need than I.

I had learned so much from George Mereshian that I grew to enjoy calling on the sick and visiting people in their homes. I discovered an evangelical Christian home for the aged ladies and decided that I would be their pastor. I never told anyone I saw it that way, but I took it upon myself to round up some buddies, and we went there every Saturday for three years and held services for them.

It was good practice. I taught them the Word, led hymns, organized the program with the other talent available, and even took them gifts of clothes and food. This was my little parish, and I loved it—not just the experience, but the dear older women, too.

I really tried to get to know them. They had their own particular needs. One night an old French woman's aged sister died, and the woman asked if I would sit with her by the casket through the night, as is the custom. As we sat there, just the two of us with the quite-dead sister, the woman said, "Luis, in France we have a custom, and I promised my sister I would carry it through."

"Oh?" I said. "What's that?"

"We've always been afraid of being buried alive, so I promised my sister that if she died before I did, I would make sure she was dead. The custom is to flex the muscle, and if there is no reflex, you can be sure the person is dead."

"Well then, let's just tap her knee the way doctors do," I suggested.

"That wouldn't be good enough. She could be alive and still not respond if she's just unconscious."

"What do you want to do, then?"

She pulled a long straight pin out of her hair. "If we stick this deep into the sole of her foot and she doesn't respond, then I'll be sure. But she's my sister, and I just can't bring myself to do it. Would you do it, please?"

"Oh, Lord," I prayed silently. "The things people ask you to do. . . ." There was no way around it. The woman had been dead several hours, but that didn't make it any easier. I lifted her foot and plunged in the pin. It slid as if through butter, right to the bone.

There was no movement. "Now I know she's with the Lord," the grateful woman said, giving me a kiss. "Thank you, Luis."

"Certainly," I muttered.

There were still frustrations. The weekly prayer meetings had fallen apart. I was saying the same words and reading the books, but my preaching seemed to have no power. I was prepared, psyched up, prayed up, backed up, and zealous. Yet I saw no immediate fruit.

Nothing I did seemed to make any difference. I had just about had it. I was inspired by things I read and heard about Billy Graham's ministry, but it seemed obvious I didn't have what he had.

Finally I gave God a deadline. I felt I had been in the wilderness long enough. If He had been trying to teach me humility, I guess I had learned it. Actually, I couldn't understand why He was withholding His blessing from my preaching. But I felt beaten.

I told the Lord that if I didn't see converts through my preaching by the end of the year, I would quit preaching. I would still be an active Christian, and I would still study and pray and read, but I would resign myself to simply assisting others. There was no sense preaching evangelistically if no one was coming to Christ.

The end of the year came and went about six weeks later, and I was really low. God had had His chance to prove Himself to me; I had given Him plenty of time. My mind was made up. I was through as a preacher. Who needed it? Obviously I wasn't filled, called, or gifted.

On Saturday morning, about four days into the new year, I bought a Spanish translation of Billy Graham's *The Secret of Happiness,* shut the door so I wouldn't be distracted by my sisters and their friends in the kitchen, and curled up on the couch to read.

As low as I was, I was blessed by Billy's thoughts on the Beatitudes, from Matthew 5. Though depressed and feeling starved for spiritual fruit, my learning techniques kicked into gear and I couldn't help memorizing the points he made on each Beatitude. The book didn't quite make me happy, for I was still mourning the loss of my preaching ministry, but I gained a few things from it.

That night the Brethren had what is called a cottage meeting, run by the elders, at someone's house. I didn't feel like going, but I always went out of loyalty to the elders. Someone would be preaching the Word, and it was only right to support him. Other elders did the same when I preached.

I dressed slowly and dragged myself out of the house to the bus stop, not even taking my Bible; I would just be there as moral support, anyway. We sang several hymns, but the speaker never showed up. None of the other preachers were there, either, so I was glad I hadn't brought my Bible and wouldn't be able to preach.

Finally one of the elders came to me. "Luis, you're going to have to speak. There's no one else here."

"No, no, I don't want to preach. I'm very low and unhappy right now."

"There's no one else. You have to speak."

"Please," I said, "I am not going to speak; I don't have a message. I didn't even bring my Bible."

He gave me a Bible and demanded that I preach. He was the elder, and I was obedient. I hardly had time to breathe a prayer. As I stood I decided to just read the Beatitudes and then—without notes—see how many of Billy Graham's points I could remember from the book I had read that morning. It was really terrible, because I couldn't work up any enthusiasm. While speaking, I thought how terrible it was to be pretending.

I read a verse, repeated Billy's commentary, read another verse, repeated Billy's commentary, and so on. Finally I came to, "Blessed are the pure in heart, for they shall see God," and I added a few comments, including the fact that the New Testament also says that the ". . . blood of Jesus His Son cleanses us from all sin" (1 John 1:7 NAS).

Suddenly a non-Christian woman from the neighborhood stood and began to cry. "Well, I'm not pure in heart," she sobbed. "That means I'll never see God. Somebody help me! How am I going to find God? My heart isn't pure. I haven't been cleansed. How do I get cleansed by the blood?"

We led her to Christ right there. What a thrill that was! God really has a sense of humor. He lets me try my humanistic techniques, figuring that if I threaten to quit preaching He will certainly come through and save my talent for His use. Then, when my first adult convert does appear, it's the result of one of Billy Graham's message outlines!

What I really learned from that, of course, was something I had studied and should have known all along: The Holy Spirit does the convicting. I was just a vehicle. God used me in spite of myself, and He did it in his own good time.

As Henrietta Mears said: "To be successful in God's work is to fall in line with his will and to do it his way. All that is pleasing to him is a success."

I ignored the buses that night and walked all the way home, praising the Lord that He had chosen to use me again. Yet even though I had great convictions about preaching the Word and wanted to serve Christ more than anything, I still had these terrible ups and downs.

13

Someday My Chance Will Come

> The Lord is not slack concerning his promise, as some men count slackness; but is longsuffering to us-ward, not willing that any should perish, but that all should come to repentance.
>
> 2 Peter 3:9

During the nightly prayer meetings with others from the assembly, I started writing down the thoughts I felt I was getting from the Lord. I had pages full of notes, many dealing with my own impatience. Here we had about 130 Brethren preaching on the streets, witnessing, passing out tracts, and visiting, but were we really touching this massive city of 800,000?

There were a few evangelical churches, but we weren't making a significant impact. We weren't even touching the middle and upper classes. As the months went by we kept praying for big things, but our actions weren't matching our prayers. I thought we should quit praying or start acting. We prayed, "Lord bless the work," and we had thirty children in the outreach Good News Clubs.

I thought we should do something for widows and orphans, the way the Bible said. We needed to defend the people and win them to Christ. I decided that if I could choose any area in which I could do the most to affect the masses for good, it would be in evangelism. I began seeing myself as an evangelist then, while others still saw me as a young Bible teacher.

Brethren missionaries who gave me books also passed along dated copies of American Christian magazines. A copy of *Moody Monthly* in the early 1950s caught my eye. It showed Billy Graham in the 1954

London crusade and told the whole story. What an impact that had on me!

Here I had heard that the end was near and that there would be no more revival, no more great masses of people coming to Christ. The assemblies would get smaller, and we would just have to band together and defend the faith in the last days. But it wasn't true! To say that the masses weren't turning to Christ, you had to ignore what Billy Graham was doing.

I tore out the color picture of Billy Graham and pinned it on the wall near my bed. My mother said, "That's idolatry." I knew it wasn't. I wasn't worshiping Billy Graham. I admired him, yes, but to me that picture represented what God could do through a man. And it gave a boost of hope to my growing dream to evangelize millions of Latin Americans.

I prayed that God would somehow use me to share Christ with many people, and even nations. Billy Graham's ministry proved that something was happening. God was moving. There was such a thing as mass evangelism, and it excited me.

One day when I was sick, the elders came to call on me and pray for me. They were shocked to see the picture of a man on the wall, and they told me so. Still, I talked about Billy Graham almost as if I knew him. I followed what was happening, because it made sense to me.

If there were more people on earth than ever, and God was not willing that any should perish, as 2 Peter 3:9 and 1 Timothy 2:4, 5 clearly state, then many should be coming to Christ. I was enriched by these American magazines, and I was spurred to read books about Luther, Calvin, Wesley, Whitefield, Finney, Spurgeon, Moody, and Sunday.

Why couldn't we have widespread revival and see hundreds of thousands come to Christ? South America was so in need of it! It was happening in the United States through Youth For Christ and many other organizations, so it could happen here. I believed my dream was not far off.

The Brethren had difficulty accepting mass evangelism for reasons other than that they thought the Christian population would diminish in the last days. They were big on the local church and didn't believe in giving altar calls, basically because they felt that a person's decision for Christ under such circumstances might not be genuine.

A mass evangelistic crusade, on the surface at least, seems removed from the local church, though many evangelists, including myself, have since proved that it is a perfect extension and natural place of worship for the local body.

I wanted a part in proving that God was still powerful. The world is impressed by big crowds. No, I don't believe in numbers for numbers' sake, and, no, I don't believe in big crowds to show off how the hotshot evangelist can draw a crowd. A huge crowd is a credit to God.

I had been told that Moody's and Finney's converts were weak. Others told me that mass evangelism was not for our time. Still, I felt burdened by the Lord about it. Friends gave me the book *Revival In Our Time*, which discussed Billy Graham's 1949 Los Angeles Crusade, the event that contributed to what Dr. J. Edwin Orr calls the mid-century revival.

"Why can't we see this in our country?" I wanted to know. A whole nation could be turned around with only a small percentage of conversions. Mass evangelism could lift a nation's moral and ethical standards. History bore that out.

My dream from all the reading and praying I had been doing was that Latin America could be reached on a large scale for Christ. We were doing such small works—not that there is a thing wrong with any of them. I would never criticize an individual work just because it was small. But if there is room for growth—and that means more converts—then let's get to it. Let's win the thousands. Let's start new local churches.

I believe in one-on-one evangelism. I practice it. I teach it. But it can only be a complement to the greater movement. History has shown that a nation of millions cannot be converted by one-on-one evangelism, because eventually the chain breaks down and the multiplication peters out. You can prepare the groundwork, but eventually it's necessary to move the masses, sway public opinion, influence the thought patterns of the nation and the media.

A nation will not be changed with timid methods. The nation must be confronted, challenged, answered, hit with the truth. We have nothing to lose and everything to win.

People wonder if my motivation in those days was at all ego inspired. No, I don't believe I was thinking about making a name for myself. But people have choices. They can be successful; they can be failures; or they can be mediocre. Being second-rate is certainly dishonoring to God. He spews the lukewarm out of his mouth, Revelation 3:15, 16 tells us.

I accept the biblical sanction of God. I know I am ego centered. But I'm not going to spend the rest of my life beating my breast and searching my soul. But I do ask the Lord, "If I get out of hand or if I am in the way of Your greater glory, please put me down." And I have perfect confidence that He will do it.

I allow Scripture to search my soul. I would love to say that my motivation was just sheer love for widows and orphans, which was there of course. But I am sure there are mixed motives in my desire to reach nations. I will give it to God and pray He reminds me who I am and who I am not.

My integrity will not allow me to say that I live only for the glory of God. I wish that were the case, and I want it to be that way, but I'm still human. I pray, "Lord, make everything I do pleasing to You," but that prayer is only good before the fact. If I have done something dishonoring to Him, He cannot be pleased with it.

I believe in the inherited corruption of the heart. The Lord knows all my motivations, even the basest. Slowly but surely He will chip away at any vestiges that dishonor Him, so I am at peace.

It's impossible to successfully wrestle your own ego down, because when you're on the bottom, who's on top? Still you. Ray Stedman, pastor of the Peninsula Bible Church, Palo Alto, California, says you need a third force that invades you, wrestles you down, and controls you. That force is Jesus Christ. Anyone who says he has beaten his own ego is deceiving himself.

The more I prayed and read about mass evangelism, the more convinced I became that this was where the Lord wanted me. I shifted into high gear in my personal study, and since formal theological training and degrees were not encouraged by our elders, I knew I would have to be self-taught.

I loved keeping up on trends in evangelism, and I was addicted to the truth of the Word. I wanted to know theology. I wanted to know technique. I wanted to know it all.

A Navigator representative to Argentina, Norman Lewis, influenced my life, and memorization became a big part of my study. I organized my days just like a school day, breaking the morning into four one-hour periods, studying one subject for fifty minutes, taking a ten-minute break, then studying another subject. At one time I was studying three different Bible books and some general theology.

Someone gave me an old Moody correspondence course by R. A. Torrey entitled *How to Work For Christ.* I ate it up. I didn't send the exams to Chicago, but I answered all the questions and memorized every verse in the entire eight-volume course. I spent an hour a day on that course and learned much about personal evangelism. Torrey covered everything from how to lead someone to Christ to how to deal with an agnostic. It was fantastic. There were even sections on passing out tracts, having prayer meetings, and making sermon outlines.

I still use the truths learned from that course in training counselors for crusades and television campaigns.

For two years I studied several hours a day, five days a week. Many days I nearly wept in despair when I had to pull myself away from the books and go to work. Along with that were all the service opportunities through the assembly, the radio program, the speaking engagements, and the weekly prayer meetings with my young friends. Sometimes I wonder how any of us persevered through those crises of wondering whether the Gospel had as much power in our lives as it did in converting the lost, but God kept His hand on us.

I found myself often searching my heart. I would tell myself I could handle the pride if it were just mass evangelism on a local scale. One church, one town, one region—something like that. But I wasn't interested in mass evangelism in which I was the only evangelist. I was sort of forced into that kind of thinking, because it seemed so few others caught the vision. I felt that maybe I would be the only one out there doing it, anyway.

When I read about this new invention, television, in *Time* magazine, I knew it would eventually play a major role in world evangelization. I was fascinated by the technological and social possibilities of the new medium. Even in the United States it was fairly new and, in Latin America, nearly nonexistent. The magazine told how the cameras worked and how the TV personalities used TV to their advantage.

I began to pretend that my mirror was a television camera. I preached into it, looking straight into my own eyes, assuming that—

as *Time* said—the speaker looking directly into the lens of the camera gave the viewer a feeling of intimacy, that impression that the speaker is looking each viewer in the eye.

I made sure my gestures were confined to the dimensions of the TV camera while practicing, thinking, praying, wondering. I was convinced I would one day preach on television; I just wanted to be ready.

It would be years before I preached on television, but I was rehearsing in Cordoba, Argentina, South America, when television itself was in its infancy. Just as in the bank, when I read all the manuals and tried to learn everyone's job, I knew someday my chance would come, and I wanted to be ready for the Lord to use me for His glory.

14
Sleepless Nights

... be filled with the Spirit.

Ephesians 5:18

I hardly knew where to turn. There weren't enough hours in the day to do all that I needed and wanted to do. Working at the bank was getting in my way, but I couldn't just quit. I had no other source of income.

I wanted to see Latin America come to Christ on a massive scale, and while I could get very few to agree with me that it was right or even that it could be done, I tried to realistically evaluate the situation. I had no contacts, no money; hardly anyone outside Cordoba even knew who I was. All I could do was prepare and believe that one day my chance would come; God would make it happen. I didn't know how a door would be opened, but I knew one would.

Because of all the street preaching and church work I was doing, I spent a lot of time on my knees, studying and praying. It was during this time that I began to envision, during prayer, reaching out to great crowds of people, people by the thousands, stadiums full.

It was as real to me as a prophetic word. I could not shake the mental pictures, so I just knew that one day it would come.

At first I didn't know what to make of it. Was it just my imagination telling me that I wanted to be a well-known preacher? No, I decided. I believed the Lord was laying on my heart what He was going to do. It had to be Him, because I was totally bankrupt of the resources needed to accomplish something like that.

I didn't even have the full backing of my local church, let alone all the other elements that would have to fall into place before great crowds would come to hear me preach. I knew that if it was ever to happen, and if I was going to have anything to do with it, it would have to be of the Lord. I could study and work and pray and do my own little thing there in Cordoba, but past that, I was helpless without a miracle.

Some of us still-zealous young people were encouraged by the elders to go ahead and buy a large tent so we could reach people who wouldn't come to the chapel. As long as everything was done in good taste and we didn't give altar calls, it was more than all right with them.

One of the younger elders—a construction man—helped us buy the tent and set it up in one of the neighborhoods. It held a little more than a hundred people, so we held children's meetings in the afternoons and advertised evangelistic campaigns at night.

Early on, many of the Christians in the area came to support us and make the unsaved people feel more comfortable in a crowd. It was probably a mistake to get a tent that took so much work just to keep clean and in good shape, but we had fun and we learned a lot.

I studied the Torrey books to know just what to do. His counsel on giving invitations was sound, but it had been so ingrained in me that giving an altar call actually appealed only to emotions that I agreed not to do it. We had heard many horror stories about evangelists who preached for twenty minutes and then begged people to come forward for twenty-five minutes.

And then there were the aggressive preachers who would ask the people who wanted to go to heaven to stand and those who wanted to go to hell to stay seated. These apparently were men who wanted to make themselves look better by pumping up the number of conversions or at least manipulating people into making decisions. The Brethren were dead set against it, and I was, too—at least that style—although history shows that God moves mysteriously and even saves people through unwise methods.

It was thrilling to be preaching the Gospel to unbelievers, and I knew it was training for even bigger and better things. They tell me I preached loudly and gestured expansively, as if I had a crowd of 10,000. It got to the point where all I wanted to do was study, pray, and then preach, to lead more people to Christ.

I had no peace about a girl I was dating. She was a wonderful, cultured, educated person from a fine family in the church, and we were seriously considering marriage. But I just wasn't ready. I had no savings, and though, at twenty-four, in many ways I felt emotionally mature, I still got upset when things went wrong. *How can I get married when I am like that?* I asked myself.

The biggest obstacle, though, was that in the back of my mind I simply had the feeling that she was not the girl God had for me. I still felt very young, and while her family and everyone who knew us thought it would be great if we married, I began to want out of the relationship. I didn't want to hurt her, so I let it go on longer than it should have.

I probably encouraged her, simply by not ending it for a good year longer than was wise. It wouldn't be over until I went to the United States, and even then I tried to take the easy way out. It would become one of the toughest and richest lessons of my young Christian life.

There are those who say that a preacher should not use his own failures as examples in his teaching and preaching. I disagree. It would be easy to leave this story of a disappointed young woman—and her disappointed father, as you will see—out of my autobiography, but I have always tried to teach the Bible on the basis of what it says, illustrated by my own experience.

That means that I must not hide my weaknesses. I don't want people to get the idea that because the Lord has blessed me in many ways and has used me for His glory to bring thousands to the cross, I am in any way above the ordinary struggles and battles of life.

I fail. I make mistakes. I struggle with the same sins and short-comings everyone faces. There are days when I wish this weren't the case, but when I finally found the peace I had so long searched for, I learned that God doesn't take away the temptation. There are the failures. He simply assures you that He has covered it all and gives the power for future victories.

Anyway, I prayed a lot about my future with this girl, and I was not able to have peace about it. To me that was an answer from God. If you pray over something earnestly and don't have peace—in spite of the fact that everything else about the situation looks perfect—then God is trying to tell you something. Colossians 3:15 (RSV) says, "And let the peace of Christ rule in your hearts, to which indeed you were called in the one body. And be thankful." Although I didn't handle it correctly later, I had a definite leading that this was not the girl for me.

Meanwhile I was reading books about evangelists of the past and how they moved out of their own localities and into preaching to the masses. Without fail, they started as unknowns. They had no contacts, no money. They were simply used of God. God did the work through them.

George Mueller spent more time in prayer and Bible reading than anyone I had ever heard of. He had been a leading Brethren teacher in England. He never asked anyone for a dime. Perhaps there was hope for me. Just to be involved in a big campaign would have been exciting. I didn't know how soon it would happen.

Having been named general co-secretary of a national youth congress, I was invited to meet Jim Savage, a former Youth For Christ man, president of a seminary, and a representative of the Billy Graham Association. I could hardly believe it. I was invited to a meeting of 1,100 church leaders, where we would see films of Billy preaching and would then discuss whether we could sponsor his coming to South America for a crusade. I hardly slept nights.

My role with the youth department of the assembly had given me more of a national platform, especially for speaking to young people, but I had been disappointed, too. Here I found that even some of the well-known speakers and Bible teachers we brought in could be dynamite with a message and then turn right around and put down a fellow preacher as soon as they were off the platform.

There were those, of course, who didn't do things like that. But I was shocked to find out how many did. In fact, I was drawn into the same type of cynicism and backbiting. I found that many people loved to hear me put down the others and said so, but that quickly led to another roller-coaster experience of guilt for me.

I knew I was on the wrong track with that approach, even though it was giving me entree to larger, wider audiences. One of the reasons I didn't want that kind of reputation was because, down deep, it wasn't really me. What I wanted to do was glorify God and call people to Christ. I didn't want to put people down. For one thing, I wasn't sure anymore that our own group was the only one with the answers.

I had gone for so long reading nothing but our literature that when I finally branched out and found there were evangelical leaders in many groups and denominations who had something to say, it was a real eye-opener for me.

Don't misunderstand. I don't feel I ever turned against my elders and teachers under God. I learned more Bible through the assemblies than anywhere else, ever. But I was beginning to see that there were other valid Evangelicals who loved and served the Lord as much as we did. Not the least of whom was Billy Graham.

The day finally came when I joined many other church leaders in hearing Jim Savage speak about the possibility of Graham coming to Argentina. But what impressed me most—besides the size of the crowd (as big as I'd ever seen for anything evangelical, and it was just over a thousand)—was a brief film of Billy speaking to Christian leaders in India.

The film revealed an unbelievable crowd in India, but the dramatic effect the camera left was that Billy was talking directly to us. Early in his message, which was not evangelistic but directed at Christian leaders, the camera panned the whole crowd to show the tens of thousands.

Yet, when Billy got to the heart of his message, the camera zoomed in close on his face. There on the big screen he stared right into my eyes. He was preaching from Ephesians 5:18: "And be not drunk with wine, wherein is excess; but be filled with the Spirit." It was as if the crowd in India didn't exist. He was looking right at me and shouting, "Are you filled with the Spirit? Are you filled with the Spirit? Are you filled with the Spirit?"

And somehow I knew that was my problem. That's what gave me the up-and-down Christianity. That's why I had zeal and commitment, but little fruit or victory. When would it end? When would I find the answer?

I didn't know it then, but it wouldn't be until I had been in the United States for six months.

When we arrived in Bogota, Colombia in 1964, we worked with Overseas Crusades as standard missionaries, training others in evangelism and church planting.

The typically beautiful Colombian countryside as it appeared in 1965.

"Luis Palau Responde," one of two daily radio programs begun in 1965 grew to reach an audience of an estimated 14 million in over twenty countries.

Preaching in Cali, Colombia in 1966.

My wife, Pat, and I in our early days as missionaries, sharing in a street meeting in Colombia.

Despite open hostility toward evangelicals, a group of young Christians asked us to help them organize a citywide evangelistic campaign in Bogota, Colombia in December 1966.

Ten thousand paraded through the streets of Bogota, witnessing to their faith. For me, it was the fulfillment of a ten-year dream and prayer. The efforts of these young people were instrumental in opening up Colombia to the Gospel.

The Palau family during the early years.

Preaching in the pouring tropical rain during the first crusade in the Dominican Republic in 1973, a Team member shelters me with an umbrella.

Visiting with young people during the Team's 1977 Dominican Republic Crusade. Over 105,000 attended the two-week crusade which was reported in TIME magazine.

The best technique for reaching people at any level is to love them.

During most of our crusades, the Team's "Responde" television program is aired live on local and national television networks. Viewers telephone in seeking biblical solutions to a variety of problems.

I am grateful for the superb Bible teachers that the Lord brought into my life who taught and discipled me, helping me prepare for an effective Bible teaching as well as evangelistic ministry.

An evangelist must be ready to face times away from his family — times of long, hard hours of work on the road.

In keeping with the use of media to support the Team's campaigns, Forrest Boyd of the International Media Service (Washington, D.C.) interviewed me at our 1978 crusade in Uruguay.

July, 1975, it was a great privilege to share the platform with Werner Burklin, Dr. Billy Graham, and Bishop Festo Kivengere before the 8,000 young people from 47 countries who attended Eurofest '75, in Brussels, Belgium. *(Photo by Russ Busby, Billy Graham Evangelistic Association.)*

Interpreting for Billy Graham when we traveled to Guatemala to provide help to victims of the 1976 Guatemala earthquake. *(Photo by Russ Busby, Billy Graham Evangelistic Association.)*

Our Mexico '70 Crusade in the Mexico City Arena was, in many ways, the catalyst that began to focus the attention of many on what God was doing in Latin America. During the ten-day campaign, 106,000 people came to hear the Gospel messages.

Speaking at "Youthquake" in Birmingham Cathedral, England in June 1976. These meetings marked the early stages of our ministry in Great Britain.

My mother, Mrs. Matilde de Palau, was a strong influence on my Christian life. She has been able to assist in the Family Counseling Centers at several of our crusades.

It is always very gratifying to challenge college students interested in missions, as here during the 1976 Inter-Varsity Student Missions Conference held in Urbana, Illinois.

The Anglican Bishop of Llandaff joined us on the platform of the "Jubilee '77" Crusade in Cardiff, Wales.

In 1978, I appeared on "100 Huntley Street" the popular Toronto, Canada talk show.

In 1978, I was invited to speak at the National Religious Broadcasting Convention in Washington, D.C. On the left is songwriter John W. Peterson; on the right, Dr. Jerry Falwell.

The 1972 Crusade Traveling Team consisted of (left to right) Marcelino Ortiz, Edgardo Silvoso, John McWilliam, Bruce Woodman, Luis Palau, Guillermo Villanueva, Don Fults, Jim Williams.

In October, 1978, the Luis Palau Evangelistic Team formed its own organization with headquarters in Portland, Oregon. Pictured are the original board members, discussing future goals. Left to right: Duane Logsdon, Milton Klausmann, Luis Palau, Don Ward, Dr. Dick Hillis, Paul Garza.

In 1978, 400 church leaders gathered in the Glasgow Cathedral in Scotland, inviting me to speak on church growth principles and the future of evangelism. Between 1979 and 1981 we held four exciting crusades in Scotland.

In the most explosive campaign the Team has ever held, 18,916 persons made public decisions for Christ, October 15-29, 1978. The two-week three-city Bolivian crusade attracted international attention when Bolivia's President Pereda Asbun and top military and government personnel attended the Presidential Prayer Breakfast we organized.

There were many Team persons who worked on the Uruguay 1978 crusade. My mother (who stands in front of me) came from Argentina to be with us for the crusade.

A portion of the current Team in the Portland Team office. Front row (L. to R.): John McWilliam (director of Latin American ministries), Reverend Jim Williams (vice-president and director of counseling), David L. Jones (publications manager), Robert West (director of administration), Luis Palau, Ake Lundberg (staff photographer) and Stan Jeter (media director).

How thankful I am for my wife Patricia who has been such a blessing and so supportive these past 19 years.

Our family's 1980 Christmas photo: Front row (L. to R.): Stephen, Pat, Kevin. Back row (L. to R.): Keith, myself, Andrew.

Photos courtesy of the Luis Palau Team. Photographers: Ake Lundberg, Jim Williams, Joe Lathrop, Don Young.

The 1979 National Congress on Evangelism and nightly crusade meetings in Caracas, Venezuela were held in the El Poliedro sports arena, with 65,500 people attending the six-day campaign. My greatest love continues to be reaching the masses with the Gospel in this generation.

15

It's Not a Question of Call; It's a Question of Obedience

Pray at all times in the Spirit, with all prayer and
supplication. To that end keep alert with all perseverance, making supplication for all the saints.

Ephesians 6:18 RSV

Speaking engagements were becoming more frequent, and I was
being asked to speak not only at youth meetings and rallies, but also
at evening services in various churches. That is the evangelistic service in most Latin American churches, and we consider it very important.

Finally, some people were recognizing my bent for evangelism.
Then came the mounting pressures. My mom, spiritually sensitive as
ever, kept encouraging me to leave the bank and start planting
churches. She even had towns in mind that needed churches.

"Mom, how are we going to live? We have a lot of mouths to
feed!"

"Luis, you know if the Lord is in it, He will provide."

"But I don't feel the call," I said. "I don't have that final call that
tells me it would be all right."

"The call? What call?" she said. "He gave the commission two
thousand years ago, and you've read it all your life. How many times
do you want Him to give a commandment before you obey it? It isn't
a question of call; it's a question of obedience. The call He has given;
it's the answer He is waiting for."

I feared she was right, but I wasn't confident enough in the Lord to

113

D

quit my job just yet, even though I was becoming less enamored with banking every day.

One day in late 1958 I received a flier announcing a speaking engagement by two Americans, Dick Hillis, a former missionary to China and a prisoner of the Communists, and Ray Stedman, a pastor from Palo Alto, California. I was afraid it might just be an anticommunist rally, but I was curious to see a pastor from California.

I went alone to the meeting, and afterward I noticed Pastor Stedman standing by himself. I introduced myself in English and was amazed when he immediately asked me a lot of questions and seemed genuinely interested in me.

I told him all about myself, my job, my girl friend, my motorbike, and my family. "I'd like to get to know you better," he said. I thought, *This guy's all right! He really cares.* He invited me to a Bible study with a few missionaries the next morning. I was flattered.

Years later Ray told me that when he first saw me, the Lord had impressed upon his heart to see that I got to the United States. He didn't know why and, of course, didn't even know who I was. When he discovered I was actively involved in evangelism, he knew his leading was of God.

The next day after the Bible study I gave him a ride into town on my motorbike so he could do some shopping, and we talked some more. "Wouldn't you like to go to seminary?" he asked.

"It would be nice, but I'm not sure I'll ever make it. I don't have a lot of money, and my church does not encourage formal theological education."

"Well," he said, "it could be arranged if the Lord wanted it." I couldn't argue with that. "How would you like to come to the United States?"

"I've thought about it," I admitted. "Maybe someday I'll be able to go, the Lord willing." I was just shooting the breeze. It never dawned on me that a minister from the United States would be able to arrange anything like that. I thought he was just speculating.

"You know, Luis," he said, "the Lord may just will it."

The next night, after hearing Dick Hillis speak, I saw them both off at the airport. "I'll see you in the United States," Ray said.

"Well, the Lord willing, maybe someday," I said.

"No, Luis, the Lord *is* going to will it. I'll write you from the plane."

To me, Ray Stedman seemed like a warm person, flattering, and a bit unrealistic. There was no way I was going to get to the United States within the next decade. It was out of the question. If the ministers there had as little money as the ones in South America, he wouldn't be able to help me. So why even think about it?

A few days later his letter arrived with the news that he had gotten a few businessmen together who wanted to finance my trip to the United States so I could study at Dallas Theological Seminary. It was a thrill—I had read about that school; its founder, Dr. Lewis Sperry Chafer; president John Walvoord; and all its wonderful teachers—but I quickly got cold feet.

There was too much to do in Latin America. Besides, I didn't want to spend four more years in school. And who would take care of my family? I wrote Stedman back and thanked him, but refused.

He wrote back quickly, assuring me that someone from the United States would be able to provide for my family, too. It was too incredible. I didn't know how to respond, and because other exciting events began to emerge in my life, I didn't answer his letter for several months.

Procrastination had always been a problem for me, but this was really rude. I simply ignored a couple more letters, and soon my life was busy with decisions and new open doors.

I confronted the bank branch manager with a few new policies I wasn't comfortable with and told him that due to my Christian testimony, I wasn't sure I could do everything required of me. These practices weren't illegalities, but they raised some ethical questions.

I knew I was taking my job in my hands, and the manager was not at all pleased. He reminded me of all the bank had done for me and all they had planned for me. Rather than agreeing that some of the practices might be considered less than ethical and should be changed, he insinuated that I was jeopardizing my career by rocking the boat. I knew if push ever came to shove and I was asked to do or say something I didn't feel right about, I would refuse, and that would be that.

My stock in the bank dropped overnight. I was on borrowed time, and I knew it. No doubt the headquarters bank in Buenos Aires got a report on me and would begin cultivating a new foreign-operations manager. It didn't take long, however, to discover that all this had happened in God's timing.

About four days after my confrontation with the manager, I noticed an American opening a new account. I greeted him in English and struck up a conversation. He was Keith Bentson, representing SEPAL, the Latin American division of Overseas Crusades. I told him I was a Christian, too, and we had a nice chat.

A few days later, when he came in to make his first deposit, he mentioned that he would like to know about any bilingual Christian man who might want to work for SEPAL, translating English material into Spanish for their magazine *La Voz* (*The Voice*). "You've got your man," I said.

"Who?" Keith said.

"It's me." It had burst from me without a moment's hesitation. As soon as he mentioned the job, I knew it was for me.

"Oh, Luis, you'd better think about it and talk with your family. We're talking about a very, very small salary; no doubt much less than you're making here."

"I'll talk to my family," I promised, "but I'm your man. This is exciting. I'm sure it's of God."

Keith needed time to check me out, too, and this caused a few ruffles in the church. The elders didn't like the idea that I would be working with an organization that was interdenominational. A missionary lady I consulted also strongly advised me against it.

She reminded me that I had a good job and all the opportunities I wanted to serve the Lord. But I had already gotten my mom's blessing and would not be deterred. I was looking for more confirmation than advice, anyway, though I must admit I was surprised and disappointed by her reaction. It was years later that I really learned and accepted the biblical principle of more strictly following the leadership and authority of those over me in the Lord.

The only stipulation I made with Keith was that I be allowed to come in late on Monday mornings, because I had speaking engagements lined up for Sunday nights for weeks to come, and I wanted to be able to fulfill them. Some were as far away as seventy miles, and it was easier to come back the next morning on the bus.

Once we had that out of the way and I got over the shock of the tiny salary offered, I was on cloud nine. I had finally found a way to get into full-time Christian work. There was a lot to look forward to, and I hadn't been this sure about God's leading in my life for a long time.

Four days after my confrontation with the bank manager, I gave him notice. He handed me my final check, asked me to give instructions to my fill-in replacement, and then I was free. Two of my sisters had found jobs by now, so having my salary cut by more than half would not hurt the family much.

I went from being close to the top at the bank to low man at SEPAL. But I loved it. I did a little of everything, including representing the mission and the magazine at conventions. I continued my tent preaching through the church on my own time, but one of the greatest lessons and blessings of those days came from praying with Keith Bentson.

After I had been at SEPAL a few weeks, he asked me to stay at the office after closing time one Wednesday night. He didn't want other staff members to think I was getting privileged treatment. He simply wanted to pray with me.

That first Wednesday night he prayed for me and my sisters and mother, then my church and all the elders by name. I was amazed at how informed he was, since he did not attend our church. It was exciting to hear him pour out his heart, imploring, "Oh, God, bless these men for Your service and Your glory!" It made me want to pray, too, so I did.

The next week he brought a map of the city of Cordoba and pinpointed the fifteen or sixteen local churches of the Brethren movement. Then he prayed for each church, literally one by one, by name and address and names of key leaders, if he knew them. It was as if we had taken a trip around the city, on our knees.

He just poured out his soul, teaching me what intercessory prayer was all about. It was thrilling. We got into the habit of praying conversationally, back and forth, and often he paced the room as he talked to the Lord.

The next Wednesday his map of the city included all the evangelical churches of all denominations. He prayed for each one, incredibly knowing the pastor's name, in most cases. It really moved me when he prayed for other denominations. When Keith prayed for them, he confirmed something in me I had felt for years. I had always wondered why, when we were taught about oneness in Christ, that this shouldn't include devout Evangelicals of other denominations. Now I was being taught the oneness of the Body through the fervent prayers of this devoted, committed missionary.

Well, as the weeks went by, Keith's map got bigger, first to encompass the state, and then the country, and then the nation. He knew how many towns there were and what percentage of them had churches. He prayed up a storm, and I was overwhelmed anew, each Wednesday night.

The meaning of Ephesians 6:18 (RSV) began to sink in with enormous strength: "Pray at all times in the Spirit, with all prayer and supplication. To that end keep alert with all perseverance, making supplication for all the saints."

All during this time, the tent ministry was growing because my friends and I pulled in people from other churches throughout the city. I had dreamed of having an evangelistic team, but I had no money and didn't know where I was going to draw the talent to help me. One night, it fell in my lap.

After a meeting, a handsome and winsome American named Bruce Woodman asked if I needed a soloist and song leader for the meetings. He was a missionary looking for a ministry and was eager to help out. I said sure. He told me he also knew a keyboard man who had worked under New York evangelist Jack Wyrtzen, named Bill Fasig; Bill could play the organ or piano for us.

Up to that time, our music had been an accordion played by my sisters or a friend from our local church. Did Bruce and Bill ever make a difference! Bruce was a perfect emcee, song leader, and soloist. He could really get a crowd excited. He did it in the Spirit, too. And of course Bill Fasig has gone on to become a widely known artist and has played for Billy Graham through the years. In my mind, we had just graduated. Now we had a team.

I knew I wasn't that good a speaker, and I kept working at it and studying. I breathed wrong, which made it hard on my voice, but many books by the old-time preachers such as C. H. Spurgeon and A. P. Gibbs' *A Primer on Preaching* gave advice on projection, sermon preparation, and anything else a budding speaker wanted to know. Bruce Woodman finally got through to me with counsel on how to breathe from my diaphragm rather than my throat and probably added ten years to my speaking voice.

We were busy and happy and productive, and the really big break from the Lord was yet to come.

16

The Big Break

Let your conversation be without covetousness; and
be content with such things as ye have: for he hath
said, I will never leave thee, nor forsake thee. So that
we may boldly say, The Lord is my helper, and I will
not fear what man shall so unto me.

Hebrews 13:5, 6

I had long been obsessed by the idea that we just needed a break, something dramatic, to open the way for mass evangelism on a large scale. Two things happened in 1960 that could be considered breakthroughs, at least for me.

The first was that Ed Murphy joined the staff of SEPAL. He was a missionary who worked with the national church.

The second was that Ray Stedman wrote me a stinging letter, telling me that not responding to his correspondence was irresponsible and rude. He made it clear that if I wanted to come to the United States, I could. I wasn't going to be forced to attend Dallas Theological Seminary or stay anywhere for four years.

I had told Ray that one of my big objections was the idea of spending four more years in classes and being almost thirty years old when I got out. "Too many people are going to hell, for me to be spending four more years reading books," I wrote him. "I can study at home. I am disciplined, and I enjoy studying. What I need is an opportunity to ask questions of some good Bible teachers and get answers to the really tough ones I haven't been able to resolve through my own reading."

I also wanted to learn more about the United States and what made Americans tick, after all I had read about that exciting country. It was a land of success, and I wanted to know why.

Ray's point, and he was right, of course, was that I should have kept the lines of communication open so he could assure me that all my questions would be answered and the obstacles overcome.

He told me there was a one-year graduate course in theology available at Multnomah School of the Bible, in Portland, Oregon, that might perfectly suit my needs and that I could spend a few months before and after that school year as an intern at his church in California.

When he sent money for my mother as a token of what they would do while I was there and also enclosed a check to pay for my trip to Buenos Aires to get my passport, my excuses had run out. I had felt for a long time that God might want me to go to the United States to see more of the world and broaden my understanding, and now the door was wide open. I prayed about it and agreed to go.

Neither the assembly nor SEPAL were terribly excited about it, the latter basically because they feared I might never return to South America. They asked me to resign from my position with them before I left, because their policy forbade national missionaries from being sent out of the country while under their auspices. (They were concerned people might join the mission simply to leave their country to study and then wouldn't come back. Then SEPAL could be criticized for taking the national workers out of the country.)

Though reluctantly agreeing that I should go, SEPAL gave me a little sermonette on the fact that I shouldn't let the United States enthrall me. "Your ministry is down here; this is God's will for you, in spite of how attractive the States are."

A few months before I was to leave, Ray Stedman set up a meeting for me with the president of Multnomah School of the Bible, Dr. Willard Aldrich, and his wife, who were visiting Buenos Aires. Ray sent me some money and told me to show them the sights, interpret for them, and so on. It was his gift to them, but it benefited me even more. It showed me what wonderful people the Aldriches were, and it gave me a friend at Multnomah before I had even left for America—and an influential friend at that.

I had several months of service left with SEPAL before departing, and it was during the last month that Ed Murphy's strategy of church planting met with astounding success in a small town. I was right in the middle of it, and it was the perfect going-away present. If I had ever questioned the power of God, this erased all doubts.

There was just enough time left before I was to leave that nervousness had not yet set in about going so far away to a land of foreigners whom, I had heard, spoke English that was not exactly the same as what I had learned in British boarding school. I was excited, and it made me even happier and more eager in my work with SEPAL.

They were letting me do more out-of-the-office evangelistic work, including preaching. That, combined with the team work with Bruce Woodman and Bill Fasig, kept me going almost around the clock. I couldn't have been more pleased.

After much prayer, Ed Murphy and the rest of us decided upon the tiny town of Oncativo as the place we wanted to start a church. What Ed wanted to prove was that you could take a small band of Christians from a neighboring town and teach them how to plant a church in the next. If the new church was strictly planted by SEPAL, then it would be a SEPAL church, which was not the point of its efforts.

On the one hand it would be too easy for SEPAL to take the responsibility and do all the work with full-time people. But that would not allow the area Christians to exercise their gifts and do what they were supposed to do. Besides, there weren't enough full-time missionaries around to keep every new church going. We deeply believed Ephesians 4:11–13 and intended to practice it implicitly.

So the plan was to visit a tiny church in Rio Segundo and see if we could get its members excited about planting a church in Oncativo, a few miles down the road. We asked the people at that small local church if they had ever taken the Gospel to Oncativo. No one thought they had.

One of our men went on ahead to check it out, and sure enough, Oncativo appeared totally pagan. There wasn't an evangelical church anywhere. No one had ever seen an Evangelical or held a tract in his hand, as far as we could tell. Five people from the small church in Rio Segundo agreed to undergo counselor training and to go with us as we tried to plant a church in their sister town.

One of the keys to our occupation of Oncativo was the fact that we had three Americans with us: Ed Murphy, Keith Bentson, Bruce Woodman, plus the editor of *La Voz*, Daniel Ericcson. They caused a lot of excitement in the town, because people wondered what they were doing there. However, they let us nationals carry the ball.

First we asked the mayor of the town if we could represent the evangelical population of Argentina in the annual May 25th Independence Day celebration and parade the next day and say a few words. He turned us down. We asked if our musicians could then join the parade and play some national songs. He turned us down again.

Strangely, we weren't discouraged in the least. To us nationals, even making such a bold request was something new and exhilarating. We weren't going to fear rejection; we were going to plunge in. First we asked around for any foreigners or Evangelicals, figuring that they would be more open to welcoming us to the city.

We were directed to a Swiss family that was indeed happy to see other foreigners. They ran a print shop in town, and Ed Murphy asked if they might have a spare room they could loan us for a meeting the next day. They offered a storeroom off the shop but insisted upon cleaning it up for us first.

In eating with them and sharing our mission, the Spirit began to work on the heart of one of the women, Lydia. It was obvious that she was searching for God, and she was moved by what we had to say. She became the first convert in that town; she received Christ right at the dinner table. We thought of the Lydia mentioned in Acts 16:14, ". . . whose heart the Lord opened. . . ."

The next day we knocked on doors all over town, inviting people to a meeting at the print-shop storeroom. Then in the afternoon our horn-playing Americans cut loose in a public park. They played march tunes and patriotic songs, drawing a crowd of curious Oncativans. Daniel Ericcson spoke for a few minutes and then turned it over to me.

I preached on Christ the Liberator, to fit in with the Independence Day celebration, based on John 8:36. The theme was that if the Son shall set you free, you shall be free indeed. He will liberate you from your conscience, your chains, and the condemnation of sin.

Street meetings are usually pretty rough, but the people listened hungrily, and I felt a real freedom, almost as if I could have given an invitation right there. I had never done that, however, and anyway, we wanted them to come to the meeting that night; I announced when and where it would be, and then the team went to the Swiss family's home to hold our breaths and wait it out.

The room had space for about seventy-five, if we really packed them in, but we had no idea whether anyone at all would show up.

I nearly trembled with excitement, praying that God would send a few needy souls to us that evening. During my prayer I got the definite urge to give an invitation that night. It was so strong that I felt I would be sinning to disobey it. Then I just hoped for a crowd.

About seventy-five townspeople packed the place. I could hardly wait to preach, especially knowing that I would be giving the first bona fide public invitation of my life. Many of the people appeared anxious to receive Christ at the street meeting, and I saw a few of them there that night.

I preached on John 10:28, 29 (NAS): "... I give eternal life to them, and they shall never perish; and no one shall snatch them out of My hand. My Father, who has given them to Me, is greater than all; and no one is able to snatch them out of the Father's hand."

It's a powerful passage of assurance that really speaks for itself. As I neared the end I felt free to invite people to receive Christ. I gave the invitation that night the same way I have now done it for years. I asked them to bow their heads and pray along with me silently if they wanted to receive Christ.

I prayed the simple prayer of confession, seeking forgiveness and inviting Christ into the heart. Then I asked those who prayed with me to raise their hands to signify their decision. I counted thirty-five hands and nearly panicked.

So the critics are right! It is all emotion. These invitations are unfair. The people feel pressured, their emotions have been tampered with. I asked them to lower their hands.

"Let me explain again," I said, and I spent another half hour on the passage, clarifying every point, making sure they understood the significance of choosing a life with Christ. We prayed again, and I asked for hands: thirty-seven.

We held a meeting there every night and trained the new converts so they could start their own church when we left. At the end of the week seventy people had professed faith in Jesus Christ. We felt as if we had been on a journey with Saint Paul to a virgin town hearing the Gospel for the first time.

We didn't have to worry about leaving seventy brand-new Christians to flounder in their week-old faith. Besides teaching them everything we could in a week—about baptism, witnessing, music, being elders, communion, and preaching the Word—our friends from Rio Segundo had been revived themselves! They would be watchdogging the new church as if it were made up of their own sons and daughters. Which it was.

Both the churches in Rio Segundo and Oncativo multiplied themselves by planting churches in other nearby towns, proving Dick Hillis and Ed Murphy right: With a lot of work in the power of the Spirit and the blessing of God, indigenous churches would spring up.

I hardly had time to come down from that experience when it was time to leave for the United States. Many friends and my whole family saw me off at the airport in Buenos Aires for the first flight of my life. It was a tearful farewell, and my mother just couldn't get enough advice in in the few minutes we had.

As I was pulling away from her in my one-and-only brand-new black suit, she said, "Don't go into the cities, don't travel alone, watch out, don't get shot and stuffed in a trunk, and remember Hebrews thirteen, five and six!" She was worried about murder. I was worried about the plane ride.

17
California, Here I Come!

I have been crucified with Christ; it is no longer I
who live, but Christ who lives in me; and the life I now
live in the flesh I live by faith in the son of God, who
loved me and gave himself for me.

Galatians 2:20 RSV

The flight was horrible. The old DC-6 chugged up over the Andes
Mountains, then settled in lower to take the strain off the engines. I
was nervous every time we changed altitude. I learned what people
meant when they talked about milk-run flights. It seems we stopped
at every airstrip between Buenos Aires and Miami.

As we flew over the Caribbean at about twenty thousand feet I was
thrilled at the sight of hundreds of beautiful sailboats. "Look at all
those little white boats," I said in my best English. My seatmate
roused and leaned across me to look. "Those are clouds, kid," he
said.

I was exhausted, and my suit was a shambles by the time we
landed in Miami ten hours later than expected. Ray Stedman was
wrong about being sure I could get a connection, so I was glad my
brother-in-law had the foresight to give me the address of some
Cubans he knew in Miami.

No one answered when I called them, so I took a cab to their place.
I didn't know the money system, could hardly understand the cab-
bie, almost didn't get my change, and then didn't know I was supposed to tip him. I left him with about fifty cents.

I didn't even know how to call Ray collect as he had instructed,
but with help from the operator, we finally got things squared away,
and I was on my way to San Francisco on a Delta jet. Now that was
living! The airline gave away so many plastic spoons, salt packets,
and postcards I couldn't believe it.

I arrived exhausted, scared, wondering why I had come, carrying one suitcase, and still wearing that new black suit, which didn't look so new now. I had no idea how out of place a tailored, black, South American suit would look in laid-back California. The plane landed with just about enough time for Ray's wife, Elaine, to pick me up and race me twenty-five miles down the Bayshore Freeway to the Sunday-evening service at Peninsula Bible Church in Palo Alto.

And I do mean race! The speed limit was then seventy miles an hour, and I know she was pushing that at least a little. We rushed into the church after the service had already started, and I was marched right down the aisle and onto the platform, to the welcoming applause of the congregation. They thought I was so cute with my accent and my black suit; they were all wearing open-collared shirts.

I stayed with the Stedman's, and within a week I had a horrible toothache to go along with my homesickness. A dentist pulled three teeth and couldn't stop the bleeding for a week, until they diagnosed that I had a vitamin deficiency.

At least having my mouth stuffed with tea bags—and whatever other home remedies they thought might help—kept me from debating with Elaine or anyone else who tried to talk to me. For some reason I was in an argumentative mood and would discuss theology and doctrine for hours.

I had come to the States to learn, but maybe I wasn't yet ready to admit that I didn't have all the answers. Ray and Elaine and their four daughters were so patient and understanding that their harmony pervaded the place, in spite of that fiery Latin who had invaded. Ray's humor kept everyone happy, and we all became fast friends.

Ray became like a father to me and even took to calling me his son when introducing me around. He treated me like a son, too, mixing a lot of advice and counsel, and even reprimanding, with his friendship. I learned as much from Ray as from anyone in the States. Mostly, his selfless consistency, his transparency, and devotion to the Word of God were an inspiration to me. I was amazed that someone could be so steady, so even, and so sharp. I've never had cause for disillusionment with Ray, and there aren't many men anyone can say that about. I know he was disappointed in me at times, but he was always quick to tell me straight out, and I admired him for that.

I've never forgotten the lessons I've learned from Ray Stedman, just from living with him and watching his life. First was his complete lack of a critical attitude. He does not talk negatively about anyone and shuts off the first hint of it from someone else. If anyone started to speak negatively about another person, he would simply say, "My, you have a critical attitude, don't you? You'd better get that settled."

Another lesson was his extreme patience under pressure, taking it in stride when someone was late for an appointment, even with his terribly jammed schedule.

Third, I was touched by his tremendous reliance on the power of Jesus Christ. He is not a high-pressure manipulator; he's just straightforward, open, quiet, truthful, never resorting to double meanings.

Ray is not competitive or self-serving. I never saw him dress to impress or try to out-do someone. This was a good example of his Christlikeness, and I thought it was the way the Christian life ought to be lived.

Another characteristic was his interest in men. He spoke like a man, not like a celebrity. He simply talked with power and seemed more like a man who was a preacher than a preacher who was a man.

I was also impressed by his expository preaching. He's one of the best I've ever heard because he gives his sermons the study time necessary and delivers them in the most interesting, human, and often humorous ways.

Mostly, I was impressed that he was the same at home as in the pulpit. Either he never let his hair down, or he always did. There was nothing hidden, no secret life. He was a great role model.

I've often heard him say, "If your reputation is okay with the Lord, it's bound to be all right with others. And if it isn't okay with the Lord, it doesn't matter, anyway."

That summer I also learned a valuable lesson from a visiting speaker from India. He was a high government official, and I wanted to find out from him what the best technique was for getting next to presidents and government leaders. "What's the method?" I asked. "What technique do you use?"

He put his arm around me and smiled. "Young man," he said, "there are no techniques. You must just love them." At first I thought he was putting me on, withholding his secret. I have since learned that his was some of the wisest counsel I ever received.

I have met with leaders from all over the world since that time, and sometimes am tempted to slip into persuasive methods or political and diplomatic protocol before I realize that what they need most and respond to fastest is love.

Sharing the love and claims of Christ with government leaders is one of the unique aspects of our ministry. Through the years, many presidents, mayors, and other leaders have listened as we opened God's Word and shared the Gospel. "Pray for me," they often ask. "I need it."

These men, because of the pressures of their positions and the type of lives they feel they must lead to be successful, seldom feel genuinely loved. Many of them weep when I say I want to pray for them, no strings attached.

I believe that if God takes hold of the hearts and lives of a nation's leaders, that nation can be opened to the Gospel and eventually turned around to the glory of God. We've seen tremendous openings during our ministry.

Doesn't the Bible repeatedly remind us that nations that fear the Lord will be blessed by Him? (*See* Psalms 115; Deuteronomy 6; 1 Samuel 12; Psalms 25:14; Proverbs 9:10.)

Two months with the Stedmans wasn't enough time to learn the American culture—how to chat and eat and behave the way the natives do—but it was all I had before going north to Multnomah School of the Bible, Portland, Oregon. I rode there with Peninsula Bible Church associate pastor Bob Smith, who was taking the one-year grad course, too.

To this day I don't believe I've seen beauty anywhere in the world that compares with the big sky, lakes, streams, ocean, and trees along the route from California into Oregon. I was amazed at the orderliness of the traffic and the general cleanliness of the rest areas and parks. Every day I was becoming more impressed with the United States.

Multnomah is a very demanding school, and I found the first semester particularly rough. I had done a lot of reading, but not so much on biblical anthropology and the doctrine of the indwelling Christ. And that's what I needed.

I was still struggling to find more fruit in my personal spiritual life.

I was frustrated in not being able to live out the life-style I saw in men like Ray Stedman and Bob Smith and several others at Peninsula Bible Church. Their lives exhibited a joy and release and freedom that I found attractive. The more I tried for it, the more elusive it became.

That made it frustrating when our Spiritual Life class professor, Dr. Kehoe, began every class—*every* class period—by quoting Galatians 2:20 (RSV): "I have been crucified with Christ; it is no longer I who live, but Christ who lives in me; and the life I now live in the flesh I live by faith in the Son of God, who loved me and gave himself for me." I had been hurt by an old friend in Argentina, who cynically made fun of the verses on victory. When I ran across a good book on the subject, my friend said, "Well, I'd like to see how victorious that author would be if he was under a broken-down car, with oil dripping all over him."

I couldn't argue with that and fell into the same type of cynicism, mostly because I couldn't find victory myself. I figured he must be right; true victory wasn't possible. The Christian life must simply be a constant struggle. But the lives of Stedman and Smith and others didn't support that argument. I wanted what they had.

On my spiritual journey, it seemed every inch of the way was like clawing uphill and then sliding back down. Although I had experienced many times of blessing and victory, for the most part I felt the struggle was impossible, unbearable. I couldn't go on that way, especially when no one else knew about it. It was my secret, private death. I knew there was a limit to how long I could hold on, like someone hanging off the edge of a cliff, deciding that if someone didn't come soon, he would have to let go.

I was treated royally at Multnomah. The other students were nice and thought I was a friendly, winsome South American. They couldn't know the spiritual battles I was having. If I didn't care so much about serving Christ and preaching the Gospel, I might have given it up at that point.

I was getting so annoyed at the teacher quoting that same verse every day that I had to ask myself why. *It can't be a Bible verse that gets you so upset,* I told myself. *It must be you.* I decided that the verse was self-contradictory, hard to understand, and confusing, especially in English. I loved the school and the classes and the other students, but the pressure in my spirit was worse than ever. I wanted to be holy.

I still wanted to be a servant of the Lord, but the battle was raging. Really raging. How does one find rest? Ray Stedman's favorite hymn was:

> Jesus, I am resting, resting,
> In the joy of what Thou art;
> I am finding out the greatness
> Of Thy loving heart.
> Thou hast bid me gaze upon Thee,
> And Thy beauty fills my soul,
> For by Thy transforming power
> Thou hast made me whole.
>
> JEAN SOPHIA PIGOTT

I was teaching a Sunday-school class and making a lot of friends, preaching in many churches around the area, even speaking in chapel. But, in my soul, I was desperate.

I was a sincere hypocrite. People always laugh when I say that, but I truly was, and it wasn't funny. Some hypocrites know they are hypocrites and want to be that way. They want to have two lives: one to show off at church and one to be in private. I simply wanted to be the person people thought I was.

If I were to describe myself in those days, I would have to say I was envious, jealous, too preoccupied and self-centered, and ambitious to a wrong degree. No amount of wrestling with myself would rid me of those sins. And yet I tried. I knew it was terrible, but I felt despicable; I hated the idea that I was a hypocrite.

I was smug about other speakers, silently rating their illustrations or delivery against my own. That left me feeling mean and ugly and petty. I had no victory. I was defeated. Even knowing what I was like on the inside, I still thought and behaved as if I was something special, on the outside. How I wanted release!

Then on top of all that, I knew there was no guarantee of funds for the second semester. Though my grades were good, I was having trouble keeping up with all the reading in English. And though America and Americans were wonderful, I was about ready to forget it and go home.

18

What a Nice Thing to Do

> And be found in him, not having mine own righteousness, which is of the law, but that which is through the faith of Christ, the righteousness which is of God by faith: That I may know him, and the power of his resurrection, and the fellowship of his sufferings, being made conformable unto his death.
>
> Philippians 3:9, 10

Nearly three months into the first semester I told the Lord that if He didn't send the money for the second semester, I would take it as a sign to go home. I couldn't work with all the other pressures, and the lack of victory in my personal life made me wonder if I wanted to continue as a preacher, anyway.

I didn't expect anything from anybody. We had been taught it was unspiritual to ask or hint for money, and besides, who would I ask? I couldn't see why anyone should give me even ten dollars, let alone a half year of schooling. A friend of Ray Stedman's had paid the first semester, but wished to remain anonymous. With the second semester only about a month away, I was pessimistic.

Over Thanksgiving I went to Tacoma to help with a ministry to military personnel. A Christian organization had a turkey dinner for them, and a few of us students were there to chat and play games and informally share the Lord. It was a good day, but I came away depressed.

I had hit a new low. The battle was a full-fledged crisis now, and on the way back to Portland, I decided I should plan on going back to Argentina. *As soon as the term is over, somehow I'm getting a plane ticket,* I told myself.

We reached Portland on Sunday afternoon, and I checked my

mailbox for a letter from home. The only thing there was a plain envelope with my name on it. I assumed it was a graded paper.

There was no letterhead; it was unsigned; and it was typed. There was no way to tell who it was from. It read:

> Dear Luis,
>
> You have been a great blessing to many of us here in the States, and we appreciate what you have taught us. . . . We feel that you deserve help to finish your term at Multnomah; therefore, all your tuition and books have been paid for.
>
> Just check in at the business office, and they will finalize the papers. So you will be grateful to every American you have met or will ever meet, we remain anonymous.

I wish I could say I had been expecting it, but I can't. I had lost faith. Now I was beside myself with excitement, and there was no one to tell. I immediately wondered who had done it, and while I have my suspicions, to this day I don't know. All I could think of was, *What a nice thing for someone to do.*

I was buoyed up once again by God's perfect timing. So He was still with me after all. Even with the defeat and the frustration I was feeling, He wanted me to know He was there and to hang in and stay at school. He had even more good things planned for me, all during the next few weeks.

The first was that I met Pat Scofield. Actually I had met her earlier in the semester in a group situation, but neither of us made any impression on the other. She was just one of the American girls. To her, I suppose I was just one of the foreign students.

One night we had a class party at a home down the block from the school, and on the way I noticed several girls. "Are you going to the party?" I asked. They all said yes, and for some reason I said to Pat, "Can I walk you over?"

She said, "Sure." It was no big deal. We weren't even together at the party, but I became interested. She was fun and talkative and even a little loud—which I normally didn't like. People who know her today can't believe she used to be the life of the party and could really cut loose. (She denies it too, but it's true.)

I was quite taken with her. She seemed mature and smart, knew how to dress well, and in conversation I discovered that she was very

spiritually sensitive. I don't know what she thought of me at first—
she still won't tell me—but I began to look for her on campus. In
fact, my window overlooked a walkway to the cafeteria, and I
watched for her every morning and then just happened to pop out
the door when she came by.

I never studied in the library, because people distracted me, but
when I found out that she studied in the library, that's where I could
be found, too; one eye on my book and one on the girl. I didn't know
what had come over me. I had to take care of my mother, and I had
big plans. Where did Pat fit in?

I continued to ignore letters from the girl in Argentina. In my foolish, naive way, I thought she would get the hint and forget about me,
but, of course, that was not the way to handle it. If I had any doubts
about whether I was doing right by giving her up, however, they
were gone now that Pat was on the scene.

She finally caught on that I was interested, and we saw a lot of
each other. There was nothing serious between us yet, but I certainly
hoped there would be. I had been smitten, and when I learned she
was going away over the Christmas break and had a few stops to
make, I worried that one of those stops might be to see an old boy-
friend. So I let her know how I felt. It wasn't anything dramatic or
romantic, just my usual, straight-out Latin style. I wanted her to
know that she was special to me, that I cared about her a great deal,
and that I hoped we could spend a lot more time together after the
holidays.

There were still a few days before Christmas break, and I was getting anxious for it to come. I would be visiting the Stedmans again,
but mostly I was weary of my courses. My studies had been so in-
tense, and I had taken almost solid Bible-book subjects for my elec-
tives. The nonelectives were Bible classes, too, so I was really getting
my fill.

I have always loved reading and studying the Bible. But when
you're getting that much of anything every day, sometimes more of
it gets to your head than to your life. I was exhilarated about the potential with Pat, but when I thought of my own spiritual condition, I
was depressed.

I had taken to sitting in the back of the auditorium during daily
chapel, where we usually got another dose of exposition or missionary stories, and daring the speaker to make me pay attention. If he

was good, I'd honor him by listening. Otherwise I daydreamed or peeked at my class notes.

For one of the last chapel services before the break, our speaker was Major Ian Thomas, founder and general director of the Torch-bearers, in England, the group that runs the Capernwray Hall Bible School. It was a challenge to make out all his words through a thick British accent and staccato delivery, but I had an edge on the rest of the students. And when he spoke and pointed a finger that had been partially cut off, I was intrigued.

Now here's an interesting man, I thought, probably just because he wasn't afraid to use that finger for gesturing. But as soon as he had me hooked, his short message spoke to me. I had been so hungry for answers to my dilemma that I had quit wondering where they would come from. I had all but given up, but, in twenty-two minutes, Ian Thomas got through to me.

His theme was, "Any old bush will do, as long as God is in the bush." The essence was that it took Moses forty years in the wilderness to get the point that he was nothing. Thomas said God was trying to tell Moses, "I don't need a pretty bush or an educated bush or an eloquent bush. Any old bush will do, as long as I am in the bush. If I am going to use you, I am going to use you. It will not be you doing something for Me, but Me doing something through you."

Thomas said the bush in the desert was likely a dry bunch of ugly little sticks that had hardly developed, yet Moses had to take off his shoes. Why? Because this was holy ground. Why? Because God was in the bush!

I was that kind of bush: the worthless, useless bunch of dried-up old sticks! I could do nothing for God. All my reading and studying and asking questions and trying to model myself after others was worthless. Everything in my ministry was worthless, unless God was in the bush! Only He could make something happen. Only He could make it work.

Thomas told of many Christian workers who failed at first because they thought they had something to offer God. He himself had once imagined that because he was an aggressive, winsome, evangelistic sort, God could use him. But God didn't use him until he came to the end of himself. I thought, *That's exactly my situation. I am at the end of myself.*

When Thomas closed out with Galatians 2:20, it all came together.

"I have been crucified with Christ; it is no longer I who live, but Christ who lives in me; and the life I now live in the flesh I live by faith in the Son of God, who loved me and gave Himself for me" (RSV).

You can't imagine the complete release I felt as a result of that little chapel talk. Years of searching had come to an end. There would be many, many more problems that had to be worked out on the basis of the principle in Galatians 2:20, but my biggest spiritual struggle was finally over. I would let God be God and Luis Palau be dependent upon Him.

I ran back to my room in tears and fell to my knees next to my bunk. I prayed in my native Spanish. "Lord, now I get it," I said. "I understand. I see the light at the end of the tunnel. The whole thing is 'not I, but Christ in me.' It's not what I'm going to do for You but rather what You're going to do through me."

I stayed on my knees until lunchtime an hour and a half later, skipping my next class to stay in communion with the Lord. I realized that the reason I hated myself inside was because I wrongly loved myself outside. I asked God's forgiveness for my pride in thinking I was a step above my countrymen because I had been well educated and could read English, because I had spent so much time with Mr. Mereshian and prayed with Keith Bentson and worked in a bank and spoken on the radio and in a tent and in churches, and I got to come to the United States and mingle with pastors and Bible-school presidents. Oh, I was really something; but God was not active in the bush. I hadn't given Him the chance.

Well, He still had a lot of burning to do, but God was finally in control of this bush. He wanted me to be grateful for all the small hinges he had put in my life, but He didn't want me to place my confidence in those opportunities making me a better minister or preacher. He wanted me not to depend on myself or my breaks, but on Christ alone, the indwelling, resurrected, almighty Lord Jesus.

It was thrilling to finally realize that we have everything we need when we have Jesus Christ literally living in us. Our inner resource is God Himself, because of our union with Jesus Christ (Colossians 2:9–15). It's His power that controls the disposition, enables us to serve, and corrects and directs (Philippians 2:13). Out of this understanding comes a godly sense of self-worth.

That day marked the intellectual turning point in my spiritual life.

The practical working out of that discovery would be lengthy and painful, but at least the realization had come. It was exciting beyond words. I could relax and rest in Jesus. He was going to do the work through me. What peace there was in knowing I could quit struggling! Theologically I knew better, but the experience made me feel I had just been converted, after trying to serve the Lord on my own for more than eight years.

Too many Christians live the way I lived all those years, because they believe that if they pray enough, read enough, and work enough, they'll be victorious. That's the essence of flesh, the essence of self. It cannot be done. We cannot work or earn our own victories through any self-effort, any more than we could work for our salvation.

I'll never forget the look on the face of an older missionary in Colombia, South America, some time later, when this truth dawned on him, too.

I'd been asked to speak to a group of missionaries at a conference during our first year on the field. My theme was the indwelling Christ as our resource and power to serve.

Afterward, this old missionary gentleman asked me to go for a walk with him. With tears streaming down his face he told me, "Luis, I have been here on the field for over thirty years. I have worked for God as hard as I could with every ounce of my being, but it's brought little but frustration. Now I see why.

"Until today, I don't think I have ever really known what it meant to allow the risen Christ to do the living in me. Thank you, brother."

My heart went out to this man, a genuine servant of the Lord, but one who had no victory in his life or ministry. His lack of victory had been evident. You could tell he was carrying bitterness and ugliness in his soul, and there hadn't been much fruit in his ministry.

What makes the difference? Perhaps it sounds too easy: Rely on the power of the resurrected Christ, rather than on self-control, where the struggle is almost unbearable. Rely on the indwelling power of the Holy Spirit, rather than on grim determination to hang on, which can be like killing yourself.

When temptation comes, turn to God and say. "Lord Jesus, You know I'm being tempted and that I cannot resist on my own. I'm relying on Your power, and I'm resting in You to turn my thoughts to something else.

"I have the mind of Christ, and therefore, with Your power, I will rely on You to give me the victory. I depend on Your strength and wisdom to serve."

That changed me, and again God's timing was perfect. My most important life decisions were approaching.

19

Go Greyhound and Leave the Driving to Me

> My brethren, count it all joy when ye fall into divers
> temptations; Knowing this, that the trying of your faith
> worketh patience.
>
> James 1:2, 3

One last gesture to prove my feelings for Pat was that I spent my
last dollar for a set of tire chains for the car she was traveling in over
the holidays. It may not have been very romantic, but I felt gallant.

I really missed her over Christmas and was anxious to get back to
school. But first there was the matter of a good lecture from Ray
Stedman. I told him all about Pat, and he wanted to know if I had
written to the girl in South America to tell her it was all over.

I told him I hadn't even written to my own mother in a long time,
but that I would get to it. That wasn't good enough for him. Every
time he mentioned it I promised I would do it, but he would accept
no promises. Finally one day he sat me down. "Look, Luis, you've
really got to write!"

Being the type of person who is tempted to put off getting a hair-
cut another month if my wife suggests I need one, my immediate
thought was, *Wait a minute. I'll write when I'm good and ready.* I didn't
say that, of course, and as you can see, in spite of my spiritual awak-
ening, I had a lot of growing up to do for a twenty-six-year-old.

"Don't worry, Ray, I'll write."

"It's going to hurt down there," he said. "The longer you prolong
it, the more bad feelings you'll cause. You should write to her father,
too, and just explain it to everyone. You could leave a trail of hurt

people if you aren't careful. It's not good, and it's not right."

"Ray, when I get back down there I'll clear it up. I'll have a little chat with them, and it'll be all over." I had gone too far. Ray had heard too much. His eyes grew cold, and he put his arm around me.

"You know, my son, you really think you can solve any problem with that mouth." I started to object, but he shut me off. "Listen to me, Luis. One of these days you are going to dig a hole so deep with your mouth that not even God will be able to pull you out of it. Unless you shape up."

That hurt. No one had ever talked to me like that. I had talked to others that way, but to be on the receiving end was something else. It really shook me up.

"I didn't mean it that way," I protested weakly.

"Oh, but you *did* mean it that way, Luis. You said you would solve everything with a little chat, and that's exactly what you meant." He loved me too much to let me get away with it. It was the first of many stiff lectures I've received in my Christian life, and while they're painful, I have grown to thank God for the men who've dished them out.

The people I most respect are the men who sat down and really had tough talks with me. I understand that kind of honesty, and I feel it's of the Lord, at least after I've had some time to lick my wounds. Ray made me face up to the fact that my ego had to be brought to the cross, especially in that situation. It wasn't enough to know the truth of Christ in me; I had to appropriate it and allow God to take me out of the way.

But Ray wasn't finished. He could tell by the look on my face that he had me, and there was more he wanted to communicate. "You are so self-confident that it oozes from your pores," he said. "Even the black suit you showed up in was designed to impress people that you were a spiritual boy. Well, God can't stand self-confident people, and He'll not use you until you are selfless. You'll be nothing, you'll go nowhere."

The interesting thing was that he was wrong about the suit. To my knowledge there was no ulterior motive for buying a black suit. I could afford only one, and I had no idea how Californians dressed. It was custom-made, but I got rid of it, anyway, since it was out of place.

I was shocked and embarrassed that he had misinterpreted my

black suit, but that didn't diminish the truth of his point. I knew he was right. I was so thankful I had seen the light after Ian Thomas's chapel talk, or I wouldn't have been equipped to deal with this tongue-lashing. It took a few days for the shock to wear off, but I wrote my letters and recorded Ray's counsel. I couldn't have forgotten it if I tried. That kind of chastisement from the Lord leaves a lasting impression.

I had waited too long to write the letters, and the girl's father contacted President Aldrich at Multnomah to complain about me. It was good that I had met Dr. Aldrich, and it was also good that he had a sensitive memory of his younger days. I admitted my mistake in waiting so long, and that was the end of it.

Another chat with Dr. Aldrich was in store, however, and it was the result of another girl-friend problem.

The second semester was exciting, although a C in Hebrews brought my grade point average down a couple of tenths of a point, to a 3.6. Pat can take some of the credit for that. I spent all the time with her that I could. By the Valentine's Day banquet, we were unofficially engaged. I didn't exactly ask her to marry me, though.

In my typical romantic fashion, as we walked under an umbrella in the Portland rain I asked her if she would return to South America with me. She knew what that entailed. And I knew what her "yes" meant, too.

Then came the problem. The policy at Multnomah was that first-year students could not become engaged. I assumed it applied to the high-school grads who were just starting. Pat and I were in our mid-twenties, and I didn't think it should apply to grad students.

The dean of men thought otherwise. I argued that I had to make decisions about applying to Overseas Crusades so we could join as soon as the school year was out, but he was adamant. We sought the counsel of people we trusted, including Pat's parents, Willard and Elsie Scofield—whom I really loved from the first—and we were encouraged to appeal the rule.

I went back, but the dean refused. "If you get engaged, you have to drop out."

"Fine," I said sharply, "then I'll drop out. But first I'd like to talk to the president, if you don't mind."

"Why do you want to do that?"

"Because I really don't want to drop out, and I don't think this merits it." We went round and round, and finally I said, "I'm sorry, but I must see the president."

I told President Aldrich that I loved Multnomah and wanted to stay, but that I would leave, if necessary, so we could become engaged. I had been offered the opportunity to apply as a missionary with Overseas Crusades to work in Colombia under my old boss, Ed Murphy, who was now field director there. First there would be missionary internship training in Detroit for seven months, and then two and a half months in Fresno to help in a Billy Graham crusade. Then there would be deputation. I was anxious to get going.

I wanted badly to be married, and I looked forward to the Graham crusade more than anything I had ever done. And I was excited by the chance to work with Ed Murphy again, with the vision of taking a Latin American country for Christ—well, Dr. Aldrich was convinced. If I waited, the whole thing would fall apart, and I would miss out on many of those opportunities.

"Okay," he said, "we'll let you do it."

In Detroit, several months later, I went over someone's head in order to remedy a situation my way, and the Lord had to teach me another lesson.

Reverend Albert Wollen, pastor of the Cedar Mill Bible Church, in Portland, rushed us through his six mandatory premarital counseling sessions, and at the end of the school year I headed back to Palo Alto to intern for two months at Peninsula Bible Church with Ray Stedman. I bought his old '55 Buick and in August, 1961, raced back up the coast, arriving just a few days before the wedding.

It had been a rough summer. We had utterly no money for phone calls, so all our contact was by mail. We couldn't dream of inviting my mother—slightly worried about this woman in my life, who was neither a friend of the family nor a Latin—to come to the wedding, because of costs. My sisters assured my mother that everything would be all right.

After we were married—with Ray Stedman sharing duties with Pastor Wollen (who is still the pastor at Cedar Mill Bible, our home church)—we took a two-week driving honeymoon down the coast, were interviewed by the Overseas Crusades board, and were accepted for missionary service. Then we hustled back to Portland to pack for Detroit.

My temper reared its ugly head in the first week of our marriage. Pat had been talking a lot about how her dad handled things—typical of a young woman reluctant to pull away—and I was starting a slow burn. Finally, on the way back she wanted me to drive straight through, rather than stop at a motel, because then she could see her mom and dad sooner.

"Well, I'll tell you what," I said. "If you want to see your father that badly, I'll put you on a Greyhound bus and you can go see him." It was cruel, and I didn't deserve a wife so patient and loving. Whenever I make a fool of myself and we both know it, she doesn't rub it in or demand an apology or go off and cry. She just leaves my comment hanging in the air to echo in my head until I'm as sick of it as she was to hear it the first time.

The trip across the country to Detroit was fun. Getting to know each other was exciting. She probably wondered what she had gotten herself into when my best-foot-forward courting approach gave way to the real Luis Palau, but she never admits that.

We visited the usual sites people see on their way across the United States, all of them brand-new to me, of course. I was intrigued by Yellowstone National Park and by the Moody Bible Institute, which we saw after spending three nights in a Chicago YMCA with a lot of strange characters. We had no money for anything better.

In Detroit for seven months of missionary internship beginning in September, we were put up in the attic bedroom of an old woman's house. The plan was that we work with a church and depend on them completely to support us. It was designed to teach us to trust the Lord for our funds and show us how to adapt to any situation. That turned out to be an understatement.

The director of the program, Mr. Fred Renich, was a wonderful man who taught us a lot at our weekly sessions in suburban Farmington. We went through several Navigator memory courses and also studied the epistles.

The problems, however, were that the church we served gave us very little, and the woman we lived with refused to put a lock on our bedroom door. She would burst in at inopportune times with a plate of cookies. It sounds funny, but you can imagine how we felt.

We were supposed to work under the pastor and do anything he asked, then he would report to the mission about whether or not he thought we were good missionary candidates. There was a lot of hard work involved, especially in an all-white church in an integrated neighborhood. Of course, the work was designed to weed out candidates who can't take a lot of thankless tasks.

It got to be too much for me, and I had thought I could do almost anything. In my mind, the project was going past the bounds of credibility. There was a box at the back of the church, into which the congregation was supposed to put any contributions for us. One week we got a quarter and a few cans of food someone didn't want. If a few friends hadn't sent five dollars now and then, I don't know what we would have done.

We couldn't go anywhere or do anything. Our waking moments were spent trying to teach classes and organize programs while literally wondering where our next meal was coming from. To me that was what this internship program was all about. Pat and I had already developed our own ideas and independence. Now we were learning unconditional obedience, and it was rough.

Jumping to the conclusion that Mr. Renich knew exactly what was going on and approved of it, I thought Overseas Crusades ought to hear about it. I couldn't imagine any rational men sanctioning missionary life at this extreme. It was time to write a letter and get this situation taken care of. Luis Palau, the man of action, was about to move.

20

The First Epistle of Saint Luis

But now ye also put off all these: anger, wrath, malice. . . .

Colossians 3:8

I fired off a hot letter to Norman L. Cummings, home director of Overseas Crusades, knowing that this would get quick action. I told him all about the situation at the church and our apartment and said, "If you don't get us out of this within four weeks, we'll pack up and go back to California. If you want us to resign from the mission, we will; we must leave this place."

Cummings, of course, immediately wrote to Fred Renich, demanding to know what in the world he was doing to this young couple. He thought, as I did, that enough was enough. Mr. Renich called us in.

I hardly let him talk, using the same resolve to leave that I had in the letter. "Why didn't you come to me and tell me before you wrote to your superiors?" he asked.

I hadn't even thought of that. "I wanted action," I said. "I figured that was the way to get it."

"Don't you see that this puts me in a bad light?" Mr. Renich said. "It makes me look careless and insensitive. I look bad with Mr. Cummings and your whole mission. Don't you think if I had known all these things, I would have taken action?"

"Well, maybe I should have come to you first," I admitted.

"Of course you should have, and frankly, I don't like it."

"But I wanted action. I've had it up to here. We want to leave."

"You don't have to go home. We're going to rectify the situation and move you next week. But first I want to tell you something." He was about to become the second man God used to lovingly let me have it. "You are choleric," he said.

Before he could go on, I was on the defensive. I had never encountered that term, and I was wracking my brain to figure out what he meant. I didn't even like the sound of the word. "What's that?" I said.

"A choleric person always wants his way. You know how to go to just the right person to get action, and in the process you don't stop to think of how many people you step on, how many you may even destroy. You don't care about that because all you care about is action.

"The problem," he continued, "is that you have a quiet wife. If you don't learn to put that choleric temperament under the control of Jesus Christ, you're going to walk all over Pat, and she just may not let you know. Then one day you'll have destroyed her, and you won't even realize it."

I was upset about not having known what *choleric* meant, but I had no argument. I was stunned, set back. I had taken it in the teeth again, and I had needed it. "Think back on your life," Mr. Renich said. "Go back to your room and think about all the people you've hurt, all the people you've stepped on, and perhaps the spiritual corpses on the side of the road you traveled to get where you are today."

I felt battered and bleeding on the way back to our apartment. One of the books we were studying covered the four basic temperaments, so I studied cholerics. It described me to a tee. It took a long time to work the whole thing out, but for the remaining several months in Detroit, I was a different person. (If you want to learn more about your temperament, I recommend Tim La Haye's *Spirit Controlled Temperament*.)

I evaluated everything I said or did on the basis of my temperament. I was amazed how it ruled me. And my memory was indeed full of people I had pushed aside without a second thought. I grew very close to Fred Renich and found him an excellent teacher. He wanted to help me learn to apply the principles of the indwelling Christ to my temperament and all my daily affairs: in marriage, in thinking, in emotions, in service, in preaching, in people relations. I had tremendous ground to make up.

The point was to control the choleric bent, not to eradicate it. I

E

couldn't change what I was, but I could bring it under control—that is, God could, in the power of the indwelling Christ. Not long after this, Ray Stedman told me that *he* was a controlled choleric. I could hardly believe it. In my mind, in basic personality he was as different from me as night and day. If a choleric could be a Ray Stedman, there was hope for me.

That internship training period turned out to be one of the most valuable seasons of my life. Because we didn't have children yet, Pat and I were able to really give ourselves to study and prayer.

An extracurricular project of mine was writing to many old friends and acquaintances to apologize for past actions. It was something I needed to do before I could feel too good about the truth I was learning about myself. It was one thing to go around happy as a lark because I was getting my spiritual life put back together, but it would be another if there were casualties still left behind.

I kept in touch with Ray Stedman during this time, so he would know that I was finally learning what he had been trying to teach me.

By the summer of 1962, we were ready to get on with our lives as missionaries. After a brief visit with Pat's family in Portland, we headed to Palo Alto, for three weeks of orientation with Overseas Crusades. While we were there, we received the shocking news that Pat's mother had contracted polio. She was stricken severely enough that she is in a wheelchair to this day. Elsie Scofield has been an amazing source of inspiration to us, in that she seems to harbor no bitterness. She never complains and is so personable that it's easy to forget she's even in a wheelchair. She's a fantastic woman. Of course, Pat hurried back to be with her for a few weeks before we had to go to Fresno for the Graham crusade.

Normally, new missionaries who have just completed orientation go immediately into their deputation work, raising the support necessary to send them to the field. But since I was to be heavily involved in evangelistic crusades and campaigns, Overseas Crusades (OC) decided it would be valuable for us to learn from the Graham team.

Actually I would have preferred to go to Colombia right after the Fresno crusade and deputation and begin campaigns as an evangelist, but OC saw that farther down the road. My mission in Colombia, like everyone else's in OC, would be to plant churches. If evangelistic preaching or a crusade-style team grew up naturally out of that, it would be considered as it came up.

I was so sure that evangelism was what I was called to that I was like a hawk at the Fresno crusade. I didn't miss a thing. I asked questions of everyone, kept a thick notebook on every detail, and learned the mechanics of mobilizing thousands of people. I tagged along with Bill Brown, the Fresno crusade director, and also visited Spanish churches in the area, inviting them to the July crusade in Ratcliffe Stadium.

Pat worked in special reservations, arranging for the large groups that come by bus and train. During the crusade itself she was to work at the counseling table, and I would interpret for the Spanish audience on one side.

At a precrusade breakfast we got to meet Billy Graham, and when he found that my ambition was to preach in evangelistic crusades in South America, he advised staying with the big cities. "Paul always went to the centers of population," he told us. "And Mr. Moody used to say that the cities were the mountains, and if you won the mountains, the valleys took care of themselves."

It was a thrill to talk to him, but I wish now we hadn't been too shy to have had our pictures taken with him. I've always been a little embarrassed by the line about my being the "Billy Graham of Latin America," but if anyone wonders why our team's crusades resemble his in many ways, they should have seen us eagerly absorbing the basics in Fresno.

Then we went immediately into deputation work all up and down the coast, speaking in churches where Ray Stedman knew the pastor, or taking any meeting OC set up.

It was a tough time and yet a rich time, because I got to know Dick Hillis. We chauffeured him to many of his speaking engagements, where he would often put Pat or me on the program first to give our testimony, then he'd preach the message himself. I believe that Dick is one of the most servantlike leaders I've ever met.

He's so much that way that when you first meet him, you wonder if he can be for real. You think, *This can't be; it must be for show.* But I've known him for nearly twenty years, and he's the same today as he was then. He's the first to help clean up the dishes or stack chairs or anything else that needs to be done. He doesn't believe he's too big for any task or any person.

I was humbled by him. Pat and I used to just sit and listen to his pithy one-liners, pieces of advice that were hard to forget. He was sold on discipling people, and I would guess that he's personally trained as many missionaries as anybody else.

He liked to emphasize "building a platform under the national." In other words, don't build a platform for yourself, build it for the national so he can speak to his own people.

He also said, "Are you worth imitating?" In other words, are you the kind of person who could say, "Follow me"? That hit hard.

Another of his lines to help with culture shock for the foreign missionary was, "It's not wrong; it's different."

If Ray Stedman is my spiritual father, Dick Hillis is my uncle. I couldn't have been blessed by two more special, godly mentors than those two. And when I think of all the other people God has sent into our lives, I praise God for His sovereign design.

Pat became pregnant during that time, and by January of 1963—though she was only seven months along—suddenly she knew it was time to go to the hospital. I couldn't believe it. We were staying in the home of some friends while doing deputation work at Valley Church in Cupertino, California. I said, "You're kidding!"

She said, "Tell that to the baby," and off we went to Stanford University Hospital.

I had been waiting in the hallway for more than an hour when the doctor, a Christian friend from Palo Alto, came and told me that there were serious complications.

"What's wrong?"

"I'm not sure yet, Luis. We just have to pray."

I was scared to death. And did I pray. There hadn't been any problems during the pregnancy, though I admit I was concerned when she went into labor at seven months. The only other unusual aspect of the pregnancy was that Ray Stedman and the chairman of the OC board kept teasing Pat that she was going to have twins. I figured if the real doctor didn't say that, who were those two amateurs trying to kid?

I couldn't sit down. I kept trying to peek down the hallway to see where the doctor was. When it was another hour and he hadn't come out again, I feared the worst. Then he showed up again. He looked worried. "We're getting an incredibly strong heartbeat for only a seven-month fetus," he said, "and it is so irregular that I must tell you I'm not optimistic."

I was nearly in tears. "Is it that bad?"

"It's bad."

"Well, save her life," I pleaded. "Can you do that?"

"Oh, yes. She doesn't appear to be in any trouble. It's the baby I'm worried about. I don't know how the baby is surviving with the heartbeat we're hearing."

I could hardly speak. "I know my wife. I don't know the baby. If you have to make a choice, save her."

For two hours I prayed with friends. I got so tired of waiting that I finally assumed that we had lost the baby. Otherwise, the doctor would have come back. The thought of that hurt deeply. I paced and paced, praying and then watching for the doctor. When he finally arrived, he wore a huge grin.

"Congratulations!" he said. "You're the father of two boys!"

I don't remember anything after that, but our friends said all I did was jump up and down. The irregular heartbeat had really been two regular heartbeats.

Kevin and Keith were premature, less than four pounds each, and had to stay in the hospital for five weeks. It drove me crazy not to be able to hold them, and I'll never forget the day we finally brought them home. Their chances had been slim for a while and their breathing difficult, but they're healthy teenagers now.

Next stop, late that same year, Costa Rica and language school for Pat. Then on to Colombia.

21

Only Thirty and Feeling Old

Now thanks be unto God, which always causeth us
to triumph in Christ, and maketh manifest the savour
of his knowledge by us in every place.

2 Corinthians 2:14

Not long before going to Costa Rica, Ed Murphy and I attended a retreat in Colombia for that nation's evangelical ministers, sponsored by World Vision International. The timing was perfect, because we were able to speak a little and get to know all the key leaders. We received an official invitation from CEDEC, the acronym of an evangelical federation in Colombia.

We considered the experience something of a spying trip, on the order of the spies' venture into Canaan in the Book of Numbers. We wanted to see if Colombia was a land of giants and/or flowing with milk and honey. I have to admit I was frustrated, already anxious to get going, to get our teeth into some work. But we were guests. Our day would come.

I felt dangerously near thirty, all of a sudden. It was as if life were slipping away. I wanted some action, to get moving, to see souls saved.

After a brief visit in the States, the family and I left for language school for Pat.

My mother came all the way from Argentina up to Costa Rica to stay with Pat and the twins while I spent five weeks in Guatemala, preaching and teaching the Bible. It was an important and fruitful time for me, but afterward I determined that the family would not be separated for that long a period again, God willing. Only once since then have we been separated for longer than three weeks, and that was during the 1980 Great Britain rallies and crusades.

On the way to Costa Rica we had stopped in Guatemala for a few days and had met several key leaders who were of help during the five-week tour.

It was great for my mother to be able to meet Pat and see the grandchildren. The women hit it off well from the start, and Pat was happy to have someone she trusted watch the boys while she spent the mornings at language school and the afternoons memorizing Spanish.

In Guatemala I preached primarily in Presbyterian churches, but also in schools and special meetings. The friends I met and made there would one day allow me to return for tremendous crusades with thousands of people. In fact, I feel more welcome in Guatemala today than in any other country I have ever preached in. Guatemala is the country whose evangelical leaders feel it could be 51 percent born-again Christian by 1982.

Looking back, I suppose I was still a very grim, determined young man. Trusting and resting in the indwelling Christ gave me great peace, yet I was very serious about wanting everyone else to have what I had. It was so new and fresh to me that I can look back on my notes and remember what thrilling days those were.

When we finally arrived in Bogota, Colombia, in the summer of 1964, I knew I was expected to be a regular missionary, training nationals in evangelism and church planting.

I didn't dare tell anyone that I considered this a stepping-stone and training for crusades of the future. The goals of OC fit in perfectly with my dreams of mass evangelism, and the mission has always been biblical and flexible, so I saw little conflict. I needed the experience, so I was willing to start from scratch.

We started with what we called local church mobilization campaigns. The idea was that we should try to be catalysts to bring together the Body of Christ and stimulate evangelism. We wanted the man in the pew to learn how to share his faith, lead others to Christ, disciple them, and plant new churches.

This was basically the reason OC was formed. We felt that the more quickly we could mobilize the church, the more progress we could make in fulfilling the Great Commission. The basic theme or motto Dick Hillis placed before us was "to stimulate and mobilize the body of Christ to continuous, effective evangelism."

The idea was to set up an office in the best possible location so that all Christians could feel confident and free to come and get acquainted with one another. We weren't in Bogota long before we began to feel that city was not the best place for our headquarters. Ed Murphy and I prayed for Colombia, finally simultaneously realizing that God had answered and would open the country.

I've had that experience only a few times in my ministry, but it is thrilling. You pray until you've "prayed through," and the Lord gives you assurance that He has answered and worked. You may not know how—and you may never know—but you know that He has. Daniel experienced this in chapters 9 and 10 of the Book of Daniel.

According to all reports, Cali appeared to have a more receptive climate for the Gospel than Bogota. One of the principles of effective church growth is that you go where the harvest is. That doesn't mean you despise sowing, but OC is basically a harvesting mission. We felt that the real harvest was in Cali, a town less than half the size of the capital, Bogota, which then had about 2 million citizens.

We moved around a little in Cali, finally finding an apartment and praying that we would get used to the culture. Pat never liked having a housekeeper, but one was almost mandatory to guard the house and to double as a baby-sitter when necessary.

When we settled down and began to work, our first effort was with a Christian and Missionary Alliance Church where we held Colombia's first evangelistic street meetings. My old friend Bruce Woodman—who was now working at HCJB radio in Quito, Ecuador—came and played the trombone and led singing.

I shared the preaching duties with another Argentine-born evangelist, Santiago Garabaya. It turned out he and I had the same temperament. We were a couple of wild young horses who needed to be reined in continually and corralled by Ed Murphy. What a job for a field director: two Latin evangelists anxious to get rolling in big campaigns. How Ed survived us, only God knows.

Ed always stayed in the background as the silent prayer warrior, always insisting that the nationals do the work of reaching their countrymen. We were glad to have him behind us, though, because in the first street meetings especially, the local Christians did not want to get involved. They thought we were in for rough treatment from the public and the authorities. The situation in Colombia was touchy. Only a few years previously, Evangelicals had undergone extreme persecution for their faith. Preaching in the streets as we were doing, was very risky, if not foolhardy. But we were convinced God was going to swing the doors wide open for evangelism in Colombia. One day, while we were preaching to a small crowd, six formal religious leaders approached. One of our young guys met them halfway across the square and defused them by telling them how wonderful it was that the Evangelicals were having a meeting.

"What are they doing?" the six asked.

"They're speaking straight from the Bible."

"Oh, that is good," they agreed. And they went on their way. The current discussions over Protestants simply being separated brethren did us a lot of good in Cali.

Pat went to the meetings and baptismal services. We had wonderful times ministering together, something you lose as families get bigger and ministries require more travel. We talked for hours. I don't think we've ever gotten bored with each other. That was when she first started neutralizing my anger with her silence.

She was not vindictive or cold-shouldered. She simply would not try to argue and reason with a man who was angry. Early in our marriage I blew up at her when a walk to a park ended in our getting drenched by a rainstorm. After all, it had been her idea, and now we were soaked.

She didn't respond until weeks later, when I asked where she would like to go during some free time. "I think you'd better decide where we go this time," she said.

I praise the Lord that this was a couple of decades ago and that the Lord—along with giving me the perfect wife for my temperament—has allowed me to see victory in this area.

Pat has always been stoic. By the same token, she doesn't get carried away about the results of a good evangelistic campaign. That's just not her style. I might overhear her telling someone about it, but never bragging or acting overly impressed.

The next church we worked with was in a poor neighborhood called San Marcos. A group of fifteen believers grew to well over a hundred after we spent two weeks in revival services, evangelism, and training.

Around this time Bruce Woodman got the idea that I should occasionally come to Quito to record a daily radio program. In a year or so we would move into the television counseling program "Responde." The radio programs are still heard all over Latin America, every day, by an estimated audience of 14 million. Even when he and I quit officially working together and he was not with HCJB anymore, these programs continued to be broadcast on a growing number of stations, which gave tremendous coverage to our campaigns and helped build the base for future crusades across the Spanish-speaking world.

Our ministry in Colombia continued to be successful, by God's grace. I learned to be used in a variety of ways, but all the while I kept appealing to the home office for more action in evangelistic campaigns. When one of the board members or the president visited the field, I got him alone and pleaded with him to let me start my own evangelistic team and begin campaigning.

They admitted that they had started me small so I could learn many things, including humility, but they weren't ready to turn me loose for mass crusades just yet. Garabaya was considered the better evangelist, and I the better Bible teacher. That may have been accurate, but I felt an evangelist should also be a good Bible teacher, so it certainly shouldn't have been considered a liability.

I was now into my thirties and felt as if opportunities in mass evangelism were passing me by. I had learned a lot and had big plans, but I couldn't do it on my own. It seemed logical to me that OC should allow such a crusade team within the mission, but they weren't sure I was ready for it yet. And they were probably right.

The first church campaign I was allowed to do on my own was at LaFloresta Presbyterian in Cali, in September of 1965. I knew that if our strategy was going to work in big city-wide campaigns, it would have to work in small local churches, too. This one qualified as that. It had about sixty members.

We were invited by an American missionary who doubled as their pastor. I took team member Joe Lathrop for leading the singing and an inspiring young national, Libny Piñeda, was my right-hand man. He had been helpful in street meetings in Cali, and I found him an enthusiastic, dedicated, prayerful teenager.

He and I prayed up a storm about that two-week campaign, finally breaking through and feeling certain that God had decided to bring revival to the church. The plan was that we would follow the Keswick Bible Conference outline and spend the first week working on the Christians. We felt that the first thing to do in inspiring the church for evangelism was to make sure the Christians were walking in the light and were up-to-date in their spiritual lives.

A Christian out of fellowship with God might do the work of inviting people to the meeting and cooperating with your efforts out of a sense of duty or the realization that he will betray his spiritual bankruptcy if he doesn't. But, when he's out there on the street, rather than dying with Christ, he's more likely to be dying of embarrassment.

So I was going to preach on a different theme every night, spending the first five evenings on the possibilities of the Christian life. Libny and I read books on revival and evangelism, such as Oswald J. Smith's *The Revival We Need* and *The Man God Uses*, until we were so excited we could hardly wait. We were praying for big things.

The first night, I wanted the Christians to be tantalized by the possibilities available to them if they wished to get their houses in order, using 2 Corinthians 2:14 as a basis. Then, on the second night—Monday—I would cover the reason Christians miss out on all those wonderful possibilities: because of sin, according to 1 John 1.

I believed in the Keswick approach: If you can provoke a crisis in a man's spiritual life, you can drive him back to God. I wanted the Christians to go home from that meeting so ashamed of themselves and repentant over any carnality in their lives that they would be ready to be revived the next night.

That would be the night I would speak on the cleansing work of the blood of Christ as the remedy for sin, even in the life of the carnal Christian. The point would be to get all the guilty consciences cleansed and purified, and John 13 magnificently fit here. The fourth night was for dedication and consecration, and that would be the first time I asked for any public confession of the willingness to serve Christ anew, on the basis of Romans 12:1, 2. The last night would be on the ministry of the Holy Spirit.

The plan was precise and meaningful, and we eventually got it all in. But I nearly didn't get past the second night. God was not exactly working within our schedule. He had the fireworks planned for evening number two.

22
Breakthrough

. . . Woe to me if I do not preach the gospel!
1 Corinthians 9:16 RSV

I prepared those messages on my knees, beseeching God for revival. The first night I preached on the victory and holiness available to the Christian who is right with God. I wanted to raise their expectations of what the Christian life could be.

The second night's message was entitled, "The Spiritual Bankruptcy of the Carnal Church." I wanted people to recognize their sin and experience a spiritual crisis that would force a private encounter with their God; the next night I wanted them to come back overflowing from their experience.

First I tried to shoot down all the reasons people use to explain their carnality: their mother-in-laws, their churches, their ministers, the world, their finances, even political conditions. Then I pointed out all the sins and their root causes that keep us from God, from the tiniest to the grossest, from gossip to adultery.

That morning Libny and I felt during prayer that a breakthrough was coming, but we didn't quite expect what happened during that sermon. I was into the message and had explained the objective for the night. Then I used the passage in Matthew 5:23, 24 about settling disputes with your brothers before you bring your offering to the altar.

Starting in on the little sins, I was ready to move into the big ones that destroy homes and families, but I never got that far. Suddenly a man stood among the church's packed crowd of about two hundred. "Wait a minute!" he said. "This is enough!"

Libny, sitting on the platform behind me, immediately went to prayer. He felt, as I did, that we were about to have either a scandal or a revival. "I'm an elder of this church," the man said. "But I've got to confess my sins right here. My family is a mess, and I'm a shame to this church.

"My wife and I don't get along; my children disobey me. Look at me, I'm seated here, my wife's over there, my children are back there somewhere. Wife, come here! Children, come here!"

They came to him, weeping and broken, and people all over the tiny, steaming, crowded sanctuary began popping to their feet to confess their sins. I was speechless and scared. I wanted revival, but this was a long shot from the tradition I had grown up in. I asked for the windows to be closed and for only church members and other Christians to remain. The confession continued.

In the middle of it all, a man rose and said loudly, "My turn! You know that young man on the platform?" he announced, pointing at Libny. "I caused his father's death. He died of a heart attack, but I am responsible, because when we were both elders we had a violent personal disagreement. There's nothing I can do about it now," he said, breaking down, "but I want to ask young Libny, right here in public, if he will forgive me on behalf of his father."

"Libny," I said. "Are you going to forgive this man?" Libny went down to the man and embraced him.

What we had hoped and prayed for had happened. For nearly two hours, the congregation in that little Presbyterian church in the middle of nowhere publicly confessed its sin and got right with God. That threw my schedule off a little, but I have learned never to try to program God, anyway.

Later in the week, when we asked for a public confession of their desire to come forward and present their bodies as living sacrifices to God, almost everyone in the church did. By the end of the second week, with the Christians revived and anxious to get on with the work of evangelism, our meetings were held outside in a patio area.

Libny, Joe Lathrop, and I could hardly sleep during those two weeks. We walked around the town at night, too excited to sleep, praying, dreaming big dreams for the future. If God could do this, what else could He do? More than one hundred twenty-five people prayed to receive Christ, and about eighty joined that church. It was in a state of revival for months on end, with spontaneous evangelism and joy.

During this time, one experience shaped a crusade policy firmly in our minds and hearts.

We were to hold a city-wide crusade in a Colombian city. The meetings were to be held in an outdoor stadium, but rain was almost a certainty. In those countries, when it rains, it doesn't just sprinkle; the heavens open, and everything is quickly drenched. Many poor people would be coming, and their clothing would not be adequate to withstand a rainstorm.

We prayed, we debated, we agonized. I couldn't stand to think of all those people sitting in the cold rain. Finally, we decided to cancel the first night's meeting. But it was too late. Even after spreading the word, busloads began pouring into the city from the countryside. "But, Brother Palau, we don't mind the rain," they told me.

That night, after the meeting, we walked the streets, talking about our decision. "Never again," we determined. "We will never cancel a crusade meeting like that. We will trust God and go on."

Later that same year, I flew to Quito to try an unusual idea of live counseling on television, rather than just preaching, as other Christian TV people did. We started with a short program, but the lines were hot, and people kept calling. By the end of the nightly three-week program, we were on the air for more than three and a half hours at a time.

It was exhausting, but invigorating. From the beginning, I never wanted to be accused of breezing into a town and doing a series of evangelistic meetings, then leaving everything up in the air. Right away we opened family counseling centers to follow up callers or to deal with those who saw the telecasts and either could not get through or were too timid to call. We tried the same program in El Salvador almost five years later, and for the brief run of the program, it had better ratings than any other in that time slot.

We've found this combination of TV, the crusade meetings at the stadium, and the downtown counseling centers makes a powerful impact on a city. The question-answer format somehow causes the viewer to examine himself in the light of Scripture. We praise God for the many letters we receive after the telecasts, saying, "Mr. Palau, when you prayed with that man, I knelt in front of my television and prayed the prayer with you. *Gloria a Dios*, I feel clean again."

After the initial TV success in Quito, we began doing the program every few months, and then doing it in conjunction with crusades so people could begin to understand more of the Gospel and its relevance to everyday life. The TV viewers might come to the crusade and the crusade audience might tune in the program.

An exciting taped Christmas special, now aired on many stations, grew out of that program. For the Christmas season, the HCJB writers wrote thirty short spots, which I read as news stories concerning the events in Bethlehem and the surrounding area as if they were actually reports from Nazareth and Jerusalem and so on. It's very effective, and many stations in Latin America request the programs every December.

When our third son, Andrew, was born in Cali in February of 1966, I missed being in the delivery room because I fell asleep, and the nurse forgot to wake me up. Pat claims I didn't want to wake up for the birth, anyway, because I was squeamish. She's right; but, *really*, the nurse forgot to wake me!

The thing that gets to Pat is that if she could stay awake, why couldn't I? I tell her that I didn't have any labor pains to keep me awake. She doesn't buy the logic.

She and I were involved in ministry in exciting ways back then. We spent money we hardly had to help the churches and local groups set up cooperatives so they wouldn't starve. We even bought a sewing machine for a new convert so she could support her family with it.

One of the missionaries and I wrote to his home church in Michigan and borrowed $2,500 for some evangelistic work and promotion we felt was crucial. Our mission came down hard on us for that, and rightly so, because we had a tough time paying it back. We were earnest, I'll say that. I was getting anxious to see us turn a corner and get into some true city-wide crusade evangelism.

Undoubtedly my impatience and eagerness to get on with God's call was hard on Ed Murphy and the whole OC staff. It's a good thing they liked me and saw that I was truly committed to Christ and sharing His love. It was all they could do to keep up with their two restless Argentinian evangelists.

People were hurting. They needed Jesus Christ. I was impatient to get the message out on a massive scale in Latin America. Why couldn't people understand how important it was to be going? "Lord, let the wheels start moving . . . ," I prayed.

During Easter week of that year, Garabaya and I were scheduled for evangelistic preaching campaigns—his in Cali before 8,000 people in a covered auditorium, and mine 200 miles away in the town of Girardot, with a crowd of about 1,300. I directed the training, promotion, and publicity and arrangements for Garabaya's crusade, while someone else handled the arrangements for mine.

At the last minute, I left the preparations for his and hurried off to preach at mine. It was exciting to be involved in both. Mine was by far the largest crowd I had ever addressed, and his was bordering on the kind of mass evangelism I had dreamed about for so long. We were both excited by the response of the Colombian masses.

I preached in a Presbyterian school for four or five nights, and it was just enough to thrill me on the one hand and frustrate me on the other. It was a terrific week of evangelism and revival, but it made me want more than ever to give up everything else and go into full-time evangelistic preaching campaigns.

We were ready to aim for bigger things, but whenever I mentioned it I got the same response: "You're a Bible teacher. Be a Bible teacher. Let somebody else be the evangelist."

My reply was, "No, life is going by too fast. I want to redeem the time. I'm more than thirty years old!"

The drive within me to preach the Gospel, to proclaim Jesus Christ, was so strong that I felt, with Paul: ". . . Woe to me if I do not preach the Gospel!" (1 Corinthians 9:16 RSV). The compulsion is still there to keep on preaching to greater and greater audiences till all have a chance to hear.

So much needs to be done! Every new generation needs to hear about Jesus Christ. Years later, while preaching in great Britain, we were told that Europe is a post-Christian society.

In my opinion, either a society is Christian or it's pre-Christian. In a land that once sent missionaries to other countries, missionaries are now needed to bring its people the Gospel.

I enjoy Bible teaching. I did then and always will. But if we say that good Bible teachers don't make evangelists, then we're saying that evangelists aren't good Bible teachers. That's irrational. Personally, I prefer Bible teaching to evangelism. I felt evangelism was my duty, in obedience to the Lord, because there is such a vast need, and people are suffering. My wife and I would love for me to retire from the grueling campaigns so we could just travel together to Bible conferences where I could teach the Word in a relaxed setting. I don't know why more men don't do that, because the churches so badly need to be ministered to on a constant basis.

Anyway, it would have been easy for me to develop a complex about my evangelistic preaching. Even when I was younger, remember, everyone wanted my young friend to be the evangelist and me to be the Bible teacher. I have a hunch they didn't feel I was a good evangelist; and, you know, I probably wasn't.

I struggled over my messages. I spent hours and hours trying to think how I was going to make the people stay with me and think. I'm not the kind of evangelist who always just pulls out an old outline, adapts it to the present crowd, and gets up and talks. I'm not a natural. It doesn't come to me easily. I have to think through every aspect. Nor do I feel comfortable with just stories and gimmicks that enchant audiences but are not the Gospel.

I wanted to be an evangelist because of the command of Christ. There has long been in me a compulsion to evangelize. Evangelism also gives me tremendous authority and a platform from which to influence the Body of Christ. When I preach in a town, many pastors come for consultation on issues, and I am able to exhort and encourage the Body at large that way. I believe an evangelist has an advantage over someone who is strictly a Bible teacher, in that respect.

Now that I look back on it, and this has been corroborated in private conversations, I think the men at OC were afraid that I could not handle the glory that can go along with being a successful evangelist. They weren't sure my Latin temperament was suited to the adulation that might result from it.

Every person God has put in my life has been a blessing, especially the ones I've chafed under. These people were sent of God to disciple a sometimes over-eager young man. One, I learned later, returned from visiting the field and, hearing my "time's wasting" pitch, told the board, "We may have to clip Luis's wings."

I wanted to preach, felt called to preach, was committed to preach, and needed a team to see it happen. But the fear of God in me helped keep my ego from getting out of hand. I knew I wasn't immune to the problems that any Christian leader might have, but I truly believed that if you attempt to steal any glory from God, He'll remove His hand, and that will be the end of your ministry.

By now I was getting desperate to get going, figuring it would take several years to grow from a local church to united campaigns and beyond. If I let the years go by, I'd be an old man, still hoping and dreaming foolish dreams. I didn't want that to happen. I was ready to go out on my own, if necessary.

23

Berlin Summit

> . . . let patience have her perfect work, that ye may
> be perfect and entire, wanting nothing.
>
> James 1:4

Ray Stedman was in Guatemala for a pastor's conference, so I flew to see him. "Be patient," was his advice. It was like telling an amputee not to cry.

"How long must I sit around and sit around?" I wanted to know. "If I have to leave OC and start on my own from scratch, I may do it."

"Be patient," he repeated. "If God is in it, it will happen when the time is right."

Just before attending the World Congress on Evangelism in Berlin, late in 1966, I began getting letters from OC board member Vic Whetzel about considering Mexico as a fertile ground for mass evangelism. I had never considered it before but gave it some thought. I wasn't sure what he was driving at. Would I be asked to switch fields?

One dark, cold afternoon in West Berlin, when the congress meetings let out early and the delegates were milling around town, I received a call from OC board members Dr. Ray Benson and Dick Hillis. They wanted to take a walk with me and have a chat. We walked a long time before they got to their point.

"Luis," Dick said, "we feel you should go home on furlough in December as planned. Once your furlough is over, begin to develop your own evangelistic team with your sights set on Mexico. You'll be field director for Mexico, with your headquarters there."

For once I was speechless. A dream had come true. I am grateful to OC that they patiently worked with me. Who knows what would have happened to me or my ministry if they had let me go off on my own when I was making all that noise.

I had no connections or contacts in the States, outside my few friends on the West Coast. My major concern was whether I could have OC team member Joe Lathrop on my team. They agreed readily and asked what else they could do for me. I knew I would need a music man, too, and we arranged for Bruce Woodman to work with us, though he never officially joined the mission.

Dick Hillis told me he hoped I would "become the greatest evangelist in the world." Coming from a man who was prayerfully concerned about any potential ego problems, it was a comment I knew exactly how to take. It reflected his attitude. He wanted nothing for my glory, but all for the glory of God. So did I.

Just before leaving Colombia for Argentina—where my new family would celebrate Christmas with my original family before returning to the United States and furlough—it was time to keep a promise I had made to a band of Christian young people who wanted to make an impact on Bogota.

Ed Murphy and I had met with little success in Bogota before setting up shop in Cali, so this was an exciting proposition. This national organization of evangelical young people scheduled a parade and a four-day crusade in Bogota, December 8–12, 1966. "Even if we get killed, come what may, we'll do it," they told me, "if you'll help us." They knew it could shake up the country and open it once and for all to the Gospel.

I advised them to set high sights for Colombia, to plan a presidential prayer breakfast someday, and to work to have an Evangelical elected president one day. (Eleven years later, many of us were reunited in a Bogota hotel after the first presidential prayer breakfast for Colombia. They had waited a long time for that answer to prayer, and it was an emotional time.)

When I arrived in Bogota to help them back in 1966, I was amazed at what had already been done. Thousands of Evangelicals were coming in from surrounding towns. There were several teams of three young people each (one to preach, one to sing and play, and one to pass out tracts inviting people to the meetings) who toured the city, carrying their own boxes to stand on.

The plan was that they would slam the box down on a street corner; then the guitar player and singer would jump up and start the music, drawing a crowd. Meanwhile, the tract passer would distribute as many as he could while the speaker gave a three-minute testimony. They were through and running by the time the police came. They would run one block one way and then two blocks the other, set up the box, and do it again.

The parade was going to be a huge one. We allowed no more than four people in a row and spread them out so they stretched twelve city blocks. The kids had purchased radio time from one of the local stations, and Christian songs were played over the radio during the march. There were enough transistor radios among the marchers that the whole line could sing in unison, even though they couldn't all hear each other.

It was impressive but dangerous. The crowds began to swell. Twelve thousand people followed the parade (the next day's newspaper said thirty thousand) to the presidential plaza where, we heard later, the archbishop peeked out his window to see what was happening. Police cars maneuvered to the front of the parade to clear the streets for us. For a second I was sure we were all in for it. I even motioned for Pat to get the children out of there. The president came out and asked Libny (always on the edges of our crowds) what was going on. Libny told him and the president said, "If you can draw a crowd like this, you could get a president elected."

By the time I was ready to speak, twenty thousand people had jammed the plaza. I was beside myself.

Three hundred people raised their hands, asking for salvation, after my short message in the plaza, and several hundred more were saved during the meetings the next four nights. The young people prayed that the rain would not interfere, even though Bogota had had rain every day for more than a month.

We were spared the rain, and in fact, once the black clouds parted and allowed sunshine in during most of the service. At the end of one of the meetings, I encouraged the song leader to hurry as the clouds rolled in. Just as we finished the final prayer and people stood to leave, the heavens opened.

What a way to end one mission term and start looking forward to the next!

I had been freed of wondering about and waiting for my chance to get into crusade evangelism on a larger scale. On furlough we spread the word everywhere that Bruce and Joe and I were a new team and ready to take Mexico for Christ.

During a missions conference in Idaho, I drafted a memo to the board of OC on the goals and objectives and strategies of the Luis Palau Evangelistic Team; they haven't changed. That memo became a foundation paper for our work, stating that our objectives were: to preach Christ; to stimulate and mobilize the Body of Christ; to see hundreds, if not thousands, of young men go into the ministry; and to plant local churches.

The highlights of the next years, more than a decade, would fill the pages of two more books, and perhaps someday they will, but let me focus on events that most affected my personal and spiritual life.

For almost a year and a half we were on furlough and deputation work, finally arriving in Mexico in mid-1968. It was a rough first year, particularly on Pat and the three boys (and we had one on the way). Because of a colossal transportation snafu, we went without our own furniture for a year and a half! At one point I called my mother-in-law and encouraged her to invite Pat and the kids to Portland for four to six weeks. I said I would finance it but that Pat must not know it was my idea. I think Pat suspected, and if she didn't know for sure before, she does now.

Basically with the help of a new OC man, John McWilliam, and Joe Lathrop, we staged fourteen campaigns in Mexico in 1969 alone. The big one was in a bullring in Monterrey, where more than 30,000 heard the Gospel in nine days, with 2,000 decisions for Christ.

Although the crusade evangelism was finally launched and God was blessing with conversions, those days were some of the roughest in our ministry. Money was low and we had to wait and hope and pray that it would come in. You can learn a lot of spiritual lessons from that, but you can also find yourself living at an impractical level and wondering why.

The gigantic crusade we planned for and promoted at a baseball park in Mexico City was cancelled at the last minute by the government. We were discouraged—all of us. I wondered if we would ever get on our feet. We vowed to have that big crusade in Mexico City, somehow, someway.

Our fourth son, Stephen, was born that November, adding a nice touch to a difficult year. Good thing we both love boys!

The next year, 1970, we heard that another religious group had drawn a big crowd to a convention, so we called ours a convention, did very little advertising other than word-of-mouth, and drew more than 106,000 people in ten days. In many ways, this crusade was the catalyst that began to focus the attention of many on what God was doing in Latin America.

Through all the attacks of the enemy and the early tough going, the team and Pat and I did not lose our zeal. I was thrilled with the opportunity to present Christ to Latin America. I couldn't remember when I hadn't had that dream. And now it was happening, slowly but surely. Slow, because there was so much ground to cover, yet we kept to our excruciating schedule.

That same year Jim Williams—another new missionary and a graduate of Biola College and Trinity Seminary—joined the team. At first I had been upset because I felt he was sent without my getting a chance to interview him or get to know him. First I fired off a letter to OC, asking why they sent me a man with whom I was unfamiliar. Then when he arrived he was so quiet, and had not really learned Spanish well yet, so I wrote a complaint to Ray Stedman.

Jim soon learned Spanish fluently and became an expert in counseling, specifically family counseling. He has been with me ever since and is vice-president of the team, handling the day-to-day Latin American operations and also heading up the massive counseling centers and community-service programs required in the big crusades.

From the crusade counseling-center ministry that Jim directs, there emerged training counselors in every crusade city and an extensive counseling manual produced in Spanish and English. During every crusade, scores of people seek out the biblical advice that Jim and the counseling staff offer, and hundreds coming to Christ as they see Him as a solution to their problems.

Through the years we've added top key people, an individual at a time, until I felt we had a strong team of professionals.

We followed up new converts; we kept accurate records; we helped plant churches; we put everything on film and videotape; we wrote brochures and booklets and books; we taped radio and television programs; we set up programs for the needy; and Jim Williams continued to engineer the massive counseling programs in each city where we held a campaign.

We ministered from El Salvador to Honduras, Paraguay, Peru, Venezuela, and Costa Rica. In 1975, we held a tough but exciting three-week crusade in Managoa, Nicaragua, where the Gospel message was broadcast from one end of the Spanish-speaking world to the other through an amazing radio network. In the 70s, we began getting invitations to preach the Gospel in Great Britain and other parts of Europe. The doors just kept opening, and we excitedly kept going through them, eager to see what God would do.

John McWilliam, a graduate from San Jose State College and Talbot Theological Seminary, took over the duties of crusade director and has continued to direct the Latin American crusades. Stan Jeter, a graduate of San Jose State College, joined us to work in the area of radio and television. Reverend Marcelino Ortiz, a pastor from Mexico and a graduate of the Presbyterian Theological Seminary and Polytechnic Institute of Mexico, became a Bible teacher at the team's pastors' conferences and an associate evangelist in many of the crusades.

Bill Conard, a missionary in Latin America for fifteen years and a graduate of Moody Bible Institute and the Regent Study Course in Vancouver, British Columbia, became editor of *Continente Nuevo,* our Spanish magazine for pastors and Christian leaders. And God has continued to lead many other talented people to help us in the ministry of evangelism.

I was privileged to receive favorable press clippings throughout Latin America and was able to meet the leaders of many of the countries. All that did was intensify my love for Latin America and my desire to see every Spanish-speaking person hear the claims of Christ upon his life.

There would be meetings with Billy Graham—who has been very supportive of our ministry—and invitations to other continents, Europe and elsewhere, but as the outreach grew and became more international, I was still most moved by the contacts that reminded me of my childhood.

For a little less than two years, from 1976 to 1978, I served as president of Overseas Crusades, which I loved and was reluctant to give up when it was obvious that I could not devote enough time to both that and my preaching ministry. In October 1978, I left Overseas Crusades and set up the Luis Palau Evangelistic Team. Yet, even with all the opportunities that opened for me and the fantastic times of fellowship and work with the board of OC, my fondest memories are the ones that hit closest to home. That includes two encounters during a visit to Argentina in 1977, a visit I shall never forget.

24

Not the Pride, but the Passion

Humble yourselves in the sight of the Lord, and he
shall lift you up.

James 4:10

It's always a treat to see how my native country has changed and
also to see whether anyone remembers Luis Palau, the young
dreamer who left there back in 1960. In 1977, some of the team and I
were there for Juventud '77, an explosive youth crusade.

At one of the meetings a woman introduced herself to me, but she
didn't have to. I recognized her immediately as one of the maids we
had employed when I was a child in Ingeniero-Maschwitz.

My sisters and I had made fun of this woman because she sang a
slow, dirgelike song to the Virgin Mary to counteract all the evangelical songs my mother sang around the house. We had not been nice
to her, even though we really liked her. Years later, she told me now,
she received Christ and began attending our local Christian Brethren
assembly. She has been active there now for thirty years.

It was good to see her again, to hear her wonderful news, and to be
able to apologize for the dumb things my sisters and I did when we
were children. She and I had a good laugh over it.

On that same trip one of my aunts gave me a hymnbook Mr.
Rogers had given to my father after their first evangelistic effort following my dad's conversion. I was to preach a message in the very
chapel my dad had built and that I attended during most of my
childhood, so the gift was very meaningful to me. What memories
flooded my mind as I sat waiting to speak.

I had a lump in my throat as I saw my little nephews—who looked
so much like me more than thirty years before—sitting there on the
pews. I leafed through that little hymnbook as I waited and noticed

that Mr. Rogers had signed it, marking a page number for my father. I turned to the song.

I nearly broke into tears as my mind transported me back to Cordoba. I had been eighteen or nineteen when I suggested this very song for one of our youth meetings. I had suggested it flippantly, but as we had sung it, I remember being convicted and moved by it.

Translated from Spanish, it went something like this: "How many sheep are wandering astray? Let us go and find them in the name of the Lord. And there'll be great joy for whoever can bring them back to the Lord." It went on about sheep being caught in the thicket, and followed with a verse that goes: "What a joy it would bring us to be able to say, 'Shepherd, we have been out looking for Your sheep, and finally we've found them after a thousand trials, and here we bring them into Your fold.' "

It is nearly impossible for me to quote that in Spanish even today, because of the emotions it evokes. Somehow, I was overwhelmed by the lyrics and could hardly go on, knowing that God was calling me to find sheep that had gone astray.

Then, thirty years later, sitting in the church I had grown up in, to realize that the very song that had led me to a deeper commitment was the same one Mr. Rogers noted for my father in his gift hymnbook—it was almost too much. I found it hard to preach that day. There was no taping or photography shot that day, and it's just as well. That service stands out as clear to me now as when I was there.

That day I realized anew the impact the death of my father had had on my ministry. I want to see men and women who are in his former spiritual condition come to Christ and have their lives changed, so they can leave this earth singing as he did.

I am moved by many motivations to be an evangelist. My dream is that people from other nations will look at a country that is being revived and ask, "What is happening over there?" And also that they will get the answer: "A nation has been turned around, and God did it."

I hope mass revival can take place on this earth again, as it once did. I believe we are heading toward the climax of history and that things are going from bad to worse, but that doesn't mean we should stop struggling and fighting for the good of nations. What if the Lord doesn't return for three more generations? Or—hard as it is to fathom—thirty generations?

As I see it, we're in a last surge of evangelism in which many hundreds of thousands of new Christians are added to the fold every day. Look how many millions have been converted in just the last fifty years! There are more Christians now than ever in history. I don't think the Bible teaches a defeatist philosophy. If it did, we should have given up decades ago. I am looking for a dramatic, cataclysmic return of Jesus Christ, but until then, I will work and hope and pray for the salvation of thousands and the betterment of as many countries as possible.

I've always been intrigued by God's reaction to Abraham's petition for Sodom and Gomorrah (Genesis 18). Abraham prayed that if there were just a few righteous people left, God would spare the towns, and God agreed to withhold judgment for as few as ten. How far down the line will the Lord go in blessing a nation or city? How few righteous people does He need before He finally takes away His hand of judgment?

I believe we're going to see in Latin America perhaps three nations that will have a majority of evangelical Christians, professing biblical ethics and a love for Jesus Christ.

If that happens, I look to God to do what He promises: to send rain and harvest and healing. I don't see why it couldn't happen. It moves and excites me. It spurs me on. It's what evangelism is all about.

C. H. Spurgeon gave the challenge:

> We want again Luthers, Calvins, Bunyans, Whitefields, men fit to mark eras, whose names breathe terror in our foemen's ears. We have dire need of such. Whence will they come to us? They are the gifts of Jesus Christ to the Church, and will come in due time. He has power to give us back again a golden age of preachers, a time as fertile of great divines and mighty ministers as was the Puritan age, and when the good old truth is once more preached by men whose lips are touched as with a live coal from off the altar, this shall be the instrument in the hand of the Spirit for bringing about a great and thorough revival of religion in the land.
>
> I do not look for any other means of converting men beyond the simple preaching of the gospel and the opening of men's ears to hear it. The moment the Church of God shall despise the pulpit, God will despise her. It has been through the ministry that the Lord has always been pleased to revive and bless His Churches.

Many people think evangelists are motivated by money or ego and not by the prospect of hundreds of thousands and even whole nations turning to God. Well, no one who knows me could ever say with a straight face that I am motivated by money. Surely there are many other professions that would allow me to live more comfortably. In fact, I was involved in one before I got into Christian work.

It's not hard to understand why people suspect preachers, particularly evangelists, of ego problems. We are in the limelight. We are like the pitcher on a baseball team, alone on the mound with the ebb and flow of the game in his hand. People could think we are the stars of the show.

There is publicity and admiration and support. And, yes, there is pride to battle. Somehow Billy Graham has—in my opinion—found peace and victory over this. For me and many of my colleagues, it is not so easy. Perhaps Billy has problems in areas where others of us have found victory. I don't know. But for me at least, pride can indeed be a problem.

One of the major ways I deal with ego and pride is to remind myself just who I am and who I am not. I remember that without Christ I am nothing. When people compliment me on a message or sermon, I remember an admonition I once saw in a book. While I appreciate their kindness and enjoy the fact that I have been appreciated, I remember that, first, people don't usually think through what they're saying—they're saying it because they think it is the polite thing to say; and, second, even if they do mean it, they probably haven't heard the really great preachers of this world and thus cannot make a valid value judgment on whether or not a sermon was good.

So, while I appreciate the kindness and acceptance of people, I don't take praise too seriously. What counts is my daily walk with God. I am so conscious of weaknesses—and, thank the Lord, my team members don't allow me to forget them—that I just praise God He has blessed our work in spite of me.

Many seminary students and other enthusiastic young men say, "Luis, I want to preach to crowds; I want to be an evangelist and win souls to Christ. How did you get your big break to hold mass crusades?"

There are no big breaks in mass evangelism. God leads in many small ways, and you learn obedience each time. Big doors open on small hinges. If you feel God has called you to serve, be faithful to do everything He shows you to do. Luke 16:10 (RSV) says: "He who is faithful in a very little is faithful also in much. . . ."

Be humble. Ask God to overcome any pride and arrogance in your life. In James 4:10 (RSV) is a promise: "Humble yourselves before the Lord and he will exalt you." Seek after holiness. In Romans 12:1 we read the admonition to present our bodies to God as living, holy sacrifices. And as Robert Murray M'Cheyne said, "According to your holiness, so shall be your success. A holy man is an awesome weapon in the hand of God."

I often tell young men of the difficulties: the days and weeks away from their families, the long hours of just plain hard work. I tell them they need to study God's Word and read about the lives and work of other men and women of God. Daily time searching the Scripture and praying is a must. But, if they're serious about being used of God in full-time service, and if God is leading them, they'll find this out soon enough (1 Timothy 1:12–15; 1 Thessalonians 5:24).

Many evangelists burn out after ten years, for one reason or another. It's not always pride or any sort of sin that does them in; more often they just get tired and give up. Frankly, that is often more a temptation to me than to become proud.

Persistence is the key to keeping a youthful spirit and enthusiasm. I don't know how Billy Graham does it, but I would love to follow in his footsteps in this respect. Here he is, a grandfather in his sixties, yet he still works and acts and thinks and dreams with youthful exuberance.

I was with him in Germany a few years ago when he counseled a young man who had a team and wanted to be an evangelist. Billy told him, "Watch out for pride, immorality, and money, and be sure to walk in the Spirit."

After Billy finished encouraging him, the young German asked in broken English, "Mr. Graham, would you bless me?"

Billy could have just put his hand on the young man's shoulder and said, "God bless you," or prayed a little prayer for him; but, no, he was serious and earnest in seeking God's best for his enthusiastic young servant.

Almost as if he hadn't heard the young man's request, Billy said simply, "Let's pray." He stretched out almost prostrate on the floor on all fours. I was dumbfounded as he prayed with that young man he had known only a few minutes. He prayed his heart out, "Oh, God, bless him as he preaches Your Word and seeks to draw men to You. . . ."

I was speechless after the young man left. Billy said, "Luis, you and I are in the public eye, and most people speak very highly of us. We must follow the biblical command to humble ourselves that, in due time, God may exalt us" (James 4:10). That really touched me. Humility in private is true humility.

We have to live in the light of the cross, and that's why our team spends time in the Word every day (2 Timothy 2:15). The Bible says that some are servants of Christ and ". . . stewards of the mysteries of God" (1 Corinthians 4:1 RSV). What a privilege. This is how I want to see myself as an evangelist.

The Bible also says that it is required of stewards that they be found trustworthy (1 Corinthians 4:2). This is one of the reasons I preach on personal purity and accountability anytime I speak to Christian groups. It is the Lord who judges us, many times using people who truly love us and see weaknesses in us. If God leads them, I believe their admonitions will be as gentle as the Holy Spirit is. The Holy Spirit is not in the business of loading down servants of God with guilt.

Satan accuses through false, sometimes undefined, guilt. God points to specific sin, convicting by His Spirit and promising change as we allow Him to work.

For all that I am and do, I believe God will take care of the judging of Luis Palau. I have peace in my heart that I honestly want to do the will of God. I want to win souls.

I will continue to call men and women to Christ, and I hope to preach until my strength is gone.

> This is how one should regard us, as servants of Christ and stewards of the mysteries of God. Moreover it is required of stewards that they be found trustworthy. But with me it is a very small thing that I should be judged by you or any human court. I do not even judge myself. I am not aware of anything against myself, but I am not thereby acquitted. It is the Lord who judges me.
>
> 1 Corinthians 4:1-4 RSV

Books That Have Influenced My Life and Ministry

The Bible
Lectures to My Students, by C. H. Spurgeon
The Burning Heart: John Wesley, Evangelist, by A. Skevington Wood
Ephesians, by August Van Ryn
Revival in Our Times, by William S. Deal
God in the Garden, by Curtis Mitchell
Continuous Revival, by Norman P. Grubb
Synopsis of the Books of the Bible, by J. N. Darby
A Commentary, Critical and Explanatory, on the Old and New Testaments,
    by Jamieson, Fausset, and Brown
Hebrews, by S. I. Ridout
Spurgeon—The Early Years—An Autobiography, by C. H. Spurgeon
Jeremiah, by F. B. Meyer
Philippians, by F. Lund
The Life of D. L. Moody, by William R. Moody
D. L. Moody, by John Pollock
The Autobiography of Charles G. Finney, by Charles G. Finney and
    Helen S. Wessel
The Pentateuch, by C. H. Mackintosh
Treasury of David, by C. H. Spurgeon
The Man God Uses, by Oswald J. Smith
The Revival We Need, by Oswald J. Smith
Fundamentalism and the Word of God, by J. I. Packer
The Memoirs of Robert Murray M'Cheyne, by Robert Murray
    M'Cheyne